AF413133

Cleopatra

An Enthralling Guide to a Life of Power, Politics, and Seduction from Ancient Egypt to Rome

Free limited time bonus

Stop for a moment. We have a free bonus set up for you. The problem is this: we forget 90% of everything that we read after 7 days. Crazy fact, right? Here's the solution: we've created a printable, 1-page pdf summary for this book that you're reading now. All you have to do to get your free pdf summary is to go to the following website:

https://livetolearn.lpages.co/enthrallinghistory/

Or, Scan the QR code!

Once you do, it will be intuitive. Enjoy, and thank you!

Table of Contents

Introduction

In the annals of ancient history, there are few figures who captivate the imagination quite like Cleopatra. She is undoubtedly the most famous Egyptian ruler, but how much do we really know about the human behind the myth?

Cleopatra VII Thea Philopator was the queen of Ptolemaic Egypt from 51 to 30 BCE. She was the last active ruler of the Kingdom of Egypt before it was swallowed up by the Roman Empire. Born in 69 BCE, Cleopatra's life spanned one of the most tumultuous periods in Mediterranean history, bridging the twilight of the Hellenistic era and the dawn of the Roman Empire. Her reign, marked by political intrigue, military alliances, and romances, continues to fascinate scholars, artists, and the public more than two thousand years after her death.

Cleopatra's education and intellect set her apart from many of her contemporaries. She was fluent in multiple languages; in fact, she was the only Ptolemaic ruler to learn and converse in the ancient Egyptian language. She was well versed in philosophy, astronomy, and mathematics, thanks to her rich upbringing. This intellectual prowess, combined with her charisma and political acumen, made her a formidable leader and master negotiator.

Her education and political instinct helped her not only in fending off the Roman Republic but also in ruling over Egypt. She skillfully used Egyptian religious and cultural traditions to legitimize her rule despite her Macedonian Greek heritage. Cleopatra embraced the role of pharaoh, presenting herself as the living embodiment of Isis, the Egyptian goddess of love, healing, fertility, and the moon.

Of course, it wouldn't be a book about Cleopatra without talking about Julius Caesar and Mark Antony. These alliances had far-reaching consequences for Egypt and Rome. Was Cleopatra a harlot, using her allure to manipulate these men, or were they legitimate romantic relationships and tragedies in their own right? According to history, they have been both, depending on who was writing them. The most famous account is still Shakespeare's play *Antony and Cleopatra*, a tragedy that follows the relationship of Mark Antony and Cleopatra against the backdrop of the advancing Roman Empire. The play is not meant to be a historical record; instead, it examines themes like love, betrayal, honor, shame, and the tension between the "East" (Cleopatra's Egypt) and "West" (Octavius's Rome). The play culminates with the Battle of Actium in 31 BCE and the tragic aftermath of Antony and Cleopatra's failed defense against Rome.

We'll explore Cleopatra's life, from her early years ruling alongside her father, Ptolemy XII, to her famous romantic relationships, to the downfall of her kingdom in the face of the growing Roman power. We'll also take a look at her lasting legacy through the world of art and theater and see how these stories have colored the way we look back on her reign. We'll also put into context what the Kingdom of Egypt was like during her reign and see just how old the kingdom really was. Finally, we'll explore the unique challenges faced by a female ruler in a male-dominated ancient society.

As we explore the life and legacy of Cleopatra, we will encounter themes that resonate across history: the struggle for power, the role of women in politics, the clash of cultures, and the impact of individual personalities on the course of historical events. We'll explore how Cleopatra approached these challenges, making decisions that would be remembered, reinterpreted, and retold. Cleopatra lived in the complicated landscape of the ancient Mediterranean, so her legacy has been placed in the context of European and British history. These broad interpretations of her life change how we view it, and since it has been so long since she lived, it becomes harder and harder to find unbiased accounts that aren't colored by a particular historian's view. That being said, we'll try to take an objective look at why Cleopatra, the last ruler of the Kingdom of Egypt, was so important and why she is perhaps the most remembered and celebrated woman of the ancient world.

Chapter 1 – The Ptolemaic Dynasty: Egypt's Greek Rulers

Who Were the Ptolemies?

The Ptolemies were the dynastic family that Cleopatra belonged to. They were a Macedonian-Greek dynasty, founded by Ptolemy I Soter, the childhood friend (and possibly illegitimate brother) of Alexander the Great.[1] He later became one of his most trusted generals and advisors. Ptolemy was by Alexander's side as he conquered most of the ancient world, from the Greek islands into the Persian Empire and all the way to what is now the Punjab region of Pakistan and India.

When Alexander the Great died in 323 BCE, he left his empire without an heir, and his generals began to carve the former Alexandrian territories for themselves. It was during this tumultuous period that Ptolemy I Soter claimed Egypt for himself, taking the city of Memphis. At first, he titled himself the satrap (governor) of Egypt. In 305, he declared himself pharaoh of the Kingdom of Egypt, establishing the Ptolemaic dynasty. The Ptolemies ruled over Egypt for centuries. However, there were a few rulers who stood out from the rest. These rulers provided the foundation for Cleopatra's rule.

---

[1] Ptolemy I was very likely not Alexander's half-brother. Ptolemy likely came up with this story to provide legitimacy to his rule.

Ptolemy I Soter (305–282 BCE)

In order to legitimize his rule and make himself popular with the Egyptians, Ptolemy I established a unique approach, blending elements of Greek and Egyptian culture. He retained the Egyptian religion and had himself declared pharaoh by the priests at Memphis. This helped establish trust between himself and the Egyptians, enabling him to move the capital to the more strategic (and more Greek) city of Alexandria on the banks of the Mediterranean. He developed the city into a hub of learning and culture by establishing the Library of Alexandria, which became the biggest and most important institution of scholarship in the Hellenistic world.

Ptolemy's bureaucracy and foreign policy helped establish and defend the Kingdom of Egypt from the rulers of Alexander the Great's former territories. While he maintained Greek as the official language and staffed senior positions with Greeks, he respected Egyptian traditions and religious practices, even preserving the high priests of Ptah at Memphis. Ptolemy also made strategic alliances with the noble families in Egypt, bringing them into his court. This approach helped validate his rule among both the Greek settlers and the native Egyptians, keeping the balance of power and not showing favor to either culture.

When it came to navigating foreign policy, Ptolemy was known for his cautious and strategic thinking, a quality he had demonstrated earlier during Alexander the Great's conquests. Ptolemy engaged in the Wars of the Diadochi, the conflicts between Alexander's successors over his conquered territories, but he avoided direct military confrontations. Instead, he focused his energy on securing and expanding his control over Egypt and its surrounding territories. His successful defense of Rhodes against Antigonus I Monophthalmus in 304 BCE earned him the epithet "Soter" ("Savior"), the name by which he was referred to during his lifetime.

Ptolemy I had several wives and consorts, including the Persian princess Artakama and his mistress Thaïs. His marriage to Berenice I produced his successor, Ptolemy II Philadelphus, and in 285 BCE, Ptolemy II was made his co-regent, the first in a line of co-regents that ensured a smooth transition of power.

Ptolemy I Soter died in 283 or 282 BCE at the age of eighty-four, leaving behind a stable and prosperous kingdom.

Ptolemy II Philadelphus (285–246 BCE)

Ptolemy II Philadelphus continued his father's legacy. His reign marked the zenith of Ptolemaic power and prestige, cementing Egypt's position as a rich and dominant force in the Hellenistic world.

One of his most notable achievements was his patronage of the arts and sciences, which transformed Alexandria into the true intellectual capital of the ancient world. He expanded the Library of Alexandria, turning it into practically a legend. He also completed the Mouseion of Alexandria, an institution that served as a sort of university during the Hellenistic period. Under his rule, Alexandra became more than a strategically placed capital city. It became a hub of literary and artistic production, as Philadelphus patronized poets and writers, supporting their work and contributing to what is now known as the golden age of Alexandria.

In addition to his patronage, Philadelphus was a highly skilled diplomat and leader. He implemented a complex bureaucratic system to govern Egypt and its territories. This was influenced by the Greek system. Philadelphus oversaw the expansion of Ptolemaic rule through a combination of military campaigns and strategic alliances in the territories surrounding Egypt. He successfully expanded their influence into Asia, Syria, and the Aegean Islands, with a network of dependencies that enhanced Egypt's power and wealth.

Philadelphus took the land and influence that his father had started and improved upon it. He introduced new crops and irrigation systems to the Egyptians. He also encouraged trade around the Mediterranean. With all this innovation came the need for a new monetary system. Ptolemy II built on his father's monetary reforms, expanding and stabilizing the coinage system by issuing silver tetradrachms and overhauling bronze currency, laying the foundations for a truly monetized economy.

As a tactic to maintain his popularity at home, Philadelphus followed his father's footsteps in incorporating Egyptian customs into his rule, further cementing the unique Greco-Egyptian culture that would come to define the Ptolemaic dynasty. He continued the Egyptian tradition of ruler worship (pharaoh as a god), deifying himself and his wife (and sister), Arsinoe II, as the Theoi Adelphoi, or "Sibling Gods," drawing inspiration from both the Greek and Egyptian pantheon of gods. In Greece, Hera and Zeus were believed to be siblings and the king and queen of the gods. In Egypt, Iris and Osiris held the same role.

Philadelphus's marriage to his sister shocked Greek sensibilities, but it was already commonplace among Egyptian pharaohs. Marrying his sister served a strategic and symbolic purpose. Philadelphus could keep power within his own family and also appease the Egyptians by seeming to assimilate to their ancient traditions. By maintaining his popularity and power within Egypt, Philadelphus could focus on external threats to his land and power rather than balancing foreign diplomacy with domestic struggles. The practice of marrying siblings continued, with a few exceptions, until Cleopatra's reign.

Ptolemy II Philadelphus's reign was significant for establishing the Ptolemaic dynasty as a major Hellenistic power, transforming Alexandria into a cultural and intellectual powerhouse, and creating a unique Greco-Egyptian culture that would influence the Mediterranean world for centuries. His policies and achievements laid the foundation for Ptolemaic Egypt's golden age, setting standards of royal patronage, administrative efficiency, and cultural synthesis that would be emulated by later Hellenistic rulers and even Roman emperors.

Ptolemy V Epiphanes (205–180 BCE)

The beginning of the Ptolemaic period brought stability, prosperity, and wealth to the Kingdom of Egypt. The pharaohs expanded their territories and secured the region's economy while managing to keep infighting at bay. However, that all changed during the reigns of Ptolemy IV and V. The reign of Ptolemy V offers a glimpse into that turmoil, particularly through one of the most significant historical artifacts of the period, the Rosetta Stone.

Ptolemy V ascended to the throne at the tender age of five after the suspicious deaths of his parents, Ptolemy IV Philopator and Arsinoe III. The cause of Ptolemy IV's death is not known, though it is suspected that he was murdered at the hands of corrupt advisors who likely hoped to influence Ptolemy V's decisions. After the murder of Arsinoe III, the people of Alexandria rioted and lynched one of the court advisors who was implicated in her death. This marked the beginning of a period of instability within the kingdom, as Ptolemy V had to contend with conflicts within his court and external threats to the Kingdom of Egypt.

During his reign, the Ptolemy dynasty's rivals, Antiochus III of the Seleucid Empire and Philip V of Macedon, took advantage of the king's young age, the infighting with his advisors, and the instability in Egypt to conquer and divide parts of the Ptolemaic lands outside of Egypt. This power grab contributed to the outbreak of the Fifth Syrian War (202–195 BCE). Egypt lost much of its territory to the east, in Asia Minor and the Levant, including the highly strategic area of Coele-Syria (according to modern geography, this would be the territories stretching from southern Syria through Lebanon to northern Israel). At the same time, Ptolemy V faced a widespread Egyptian revolt that began in the southern part of the kingdom. The rebellion, led at first by the self-proclaimed pharaoh Horwennefer and later by Ankhwennefer, resulted in the loss of much of Upper Egypt for over two decades; it was only regained after a prolonged and costly military campaign.

Because Ptolemy V lost control of the lucrative Coele-Syria region, the Kingdom of Egypt had to operate with less economic power and wealth than ever before. This meant he began to impose heavy taxes on the people of Egypt, likely influencing the rebellion. The kingdom would find peace again, especially once Ptolemy V married the Seleucid princess Cleopatra I and could reaffirm his alliance with Antiochus III. However, he would not regain the power or influence Egypt had at the beginning of the Ptolemaic period.

The Decline of the Ptolemaic Dynasty

As his kingdom and influence weakened, Ptolemy V's rule gradually underscored the fragility of the Ptolemaic state. By marrying Cleopatra I, the daughter of Antiochus III of the Seleucids, he aligned Egypt more closely with the Seleucid dynasty—a move that alarmed Rome, which had recently checked Seleucid power. Ptolemy V died in 180 BCE under mysterious circumstances (he was possibly poisoned) and left behind a kingdom with a minor heir and growing internal and external pressures.

What followed over the next century was a turbulent era: the reigns of his successors (from Ptolemy VI onward) were frequently marred by power struggles, regencies, sibling rivalries, and civil strife. These internal divisions, combined with foreign threats and increasing Roman intervention, steadily eroded the strength of the Ptolemaic dynasty.

Ptolemy VIII Physcon (c. 184–116 BCE)

The most dramatic example of this dysfunction can be seen in Ptolemy VIII's reign. He was nicknamed "Physcon" (which means "Potbelly") for his obesity and reputation. He was the younger brother of Ptolemy VI Philometor. The two were supposed to rule together peacefully after their father's death; instead, they spent years locked in a rivalry for sole control of Egypt. In 164 BCE, Ptolemy VIII managed to force his brother to flee and briefly seized power, but by the following year, the opposition and external pressure forced him out. He was sent to rule Cyrenaica (modern-day Libya) as a consolation.

When Ptolemy VI died in 145 BCE, Ptolemy VIII returned to Egypt and married his sister Cleopatra II (his brother's widow), establishing himself as king. Some years later (around 141 or 140 BCE), he married his niece, Cleopatra III, the daughter of Ptolemy VI and Cleopatra II, while keeping Cleopatra II as co-queen. This arrangement, acceptable under Ptolemaic dynastic tradition, triggered deep internal tensions.

From 132 to around 126 BCE, Egypt was plunged into civil war. Cleopatra II commanded Alexandria (backed largely by Greek and Macedonian residents), while Ptolemy VIII and Cleopatra III held sway over much of the rest of Egypt, where they gained support from many native Egyptians. Ancient accounts portray Ptolemy VIII as especially ruthless. He allegedly murdered his own son, and later sources accuse him of purging opponents and driving out intellectuals from Alexandria. By the time he reconsolidated power (around 124 BCE), Egypt was politically fractured, and its institutions had been severely weakened.

Ptolemy VIII died in 116 BCE. In his will, he left the throne to Cleopatra III, with instructions that she choose one of her sons—either Ptolemy IX Soter or Ptolemy X Alexander I—as co-ruler. This set the stage for yet another round of dynastic instability and internal conflict.

Ptolemy IX Soter (Lathyros) (c. 140-81 BCE)

Cleopatra's grandfather, Ptolemy IX Soter II, nicknamed "Lathyros" ("Chickpea"), had one of the most turbulent reigns in the dynasty's history. He was the eldest son of Ptolemy VIII and Cleopatra III. When his father died, pressure forced Cleopatra III to associate Ptolemy IX with the throne, even though she appeared to favor his younger brother. She forced him to divorce his first wife, his sister Cleopatra IV, and marry his other sister, Cleopatra Selene, instead.

For a time (from 116 to 107 BCE), mother and son ruled together, but tensions mounted. In 107 BCE, his mother deposed him, and he fled Egypt. He ended up governing abroad in Cyprus. Meanwhile, his younger brother (later known as Ptolemy X Alexander) became co-ruler with Cleopatra III.

After years in exile, Ptolemy IX was recalled by the Alexandrians and restored as king in 88 BCE. He ruled again until his death in 81 BCE. During that final reign, there was unrest in Upper Egypt (including a revolt around Thebes). He did not designate an heir to succeed him. His daughter Berenice III briefly ruled, but soon a new king, Ptolemy XI Alexander II, was installed.

Ptolemy XI married Berenice III, but he reportedly murdered her just nineteen days after their wedding. The Alexandrians rioted and lynched him. Afterward, the throne passed to an illegitimate branch of the family, eventually leading to Ptolemy XII, the father of Cleopatra VII.

Environmental and Economic Collapse

On top of all this political chaos, Egypt was suffering from environmental disasters. The Nile's floods, the lifeblood of Egyptian agriculture, became increasingly unreliable during this period. When the Nile failed to flood year after year, crops failed, families went hungry, and people were forced to sell their land just to pay the ever-increasing taxes. The Ptolemies kept raising taxes to fund their civil wars and pay for Roman support, creating a vicious cycle that made the Egyptian people resent their Greek rulers even more.

The dynasty also kept losing territory. By the time Ptolemy XII came to power around 80 BCE, Egypt had long since shed most of the far-flung territories that once made the Ptolemies a great Mediterranean power. Lands such as Cyrenaica, Coele-Syria (the Levant), and other overseas holdings had slipped from Ptolemaic control, leaving the kingdom reduced largely to Egypt proper (the Nile valley and delta).

By the time Ptolemy XII sat on the throne, Egypt had suffered almost a century of chaos. The kingdom was a shadow of what it had been under Ptolemy I and II. It was economically weakened, militarily dependent on Rome, and ruled by a dynasty that had lost the respect of both the Greek and Egyptian populations. As we'll see, Ptolemy XII would only make matters worse, driving Egypt even deeper into debt and dependence on Rome, leaving his daughter Cleopatra with the nearly impossible task of restoring Egyptian independence and prosperity.

Chapter 2 – Birth of a Queen

Cleopatra VII Thea Philopator, better known to us simply as Cleopatra, was born in 69 BCE during the final decades of the Ptolemaic dynasty. At the time, the Mediterranean world was being turned on its head by the expanding Roman Republic. Cleopatra's life was marked by periods of exile and war, as well as threats to the throne from both the Roman world and within the Egyptian court. She was likely the second of five children born to Pharaoh Ptolemy XII Auletes, the others being Berenice IV (Cleopatra's elder sister), Arsinoe IV, Ptolemy XIII, and Ptolemy XIV. Her early life was characterized by an education that reflected her Macedonian Greek heritage and emphasized Hellenistic culture. Her early exposure to royal politics would inform her decisions later in life when she ruled Egypt as pharaoh.

Cleopatra's Birth and Family Life

Cleopatra's early life is still shrouded in mystery, in part because of how long ago she lived, but also due to the Roman effort to discredit her after her death. We know that she was the daughter of Ptolemy XII. She was likely not the eldest, though the exact birth order remains unclear. Her mother is believed to have been Cleopatra V Tryphaena, but that is difficult to confirm. If her mother had been Cleopatra V, some wonder whether Cleopatra should have been numbered Cleopatra VI instead of VII. However, these numeric designations are modern conventions, not ancient ones, so they were not consistently applied in antiquity. Some historians once speculated that Cleopatra VI Tryphaena might have been either identical to Cleopatra V or a separate daughter of Ptolemy

XII, possibly a co-ruler with Berenice IV. This confusion reflects the limited and often contradictory sources from this period, as well as the common reuse of royal names in the Ptolemaic dynasty. Whether Cleopatra V and VI were the same person or distinct individuals does not change the complex relationships among Cleopatra VII, her siblings, and her father.

A Hellenistic depiction of Ptolemy XII. [1]

Siblings and Status

The relationships Cleopatra had with her siblings weren't what we would consider "typical" by today's standards. In Ptolemaic Egypt, it was customary for members of the royal family to marry their siblings and rule as co-regents. This practice became a hallmark of the Ptolemaic dynasty and was intended to preserve dynastic purity and reinforce legitimacy. Although the idea may seem strange today, these sibling relationships were typically formal and politically driven rather than affectionate. They were often marked by rivalry and a continuous struggle for power.

We will talk about this in more detail, but over the course of her life, Cleopatra either opposed or outlasted all of her siblings. Berenice IV was executed by their father, Ptolemy XII, upon his return to power. Cleopatra later co-ruled with her younger brothers, Ptolemy XIII and Ptolemy XIV, both of whom died under suspicious circumstances— Ptolemy XIII drowned during a civil war, and Ptolemy XIV was likely poisoned, possibly on Cleopatra's order. Arsinoe IV, her younger sister, was executed in Ephesus years later on Cleopatra's command. Each sibling presented a potential threat to Cleopatra's rule, and the political environment of the Ptolemaic court offered little room for family loyalty.

Her path to power changed dramatically after her father's exile and the ascension of Berenice IV to the throne in his absence. Early in life, Cleopatra might have been expected to marry a foreign or dynastic ally, as royal daughters often served diplomatic roles in marriage. However, with the death of Berenice and her father's restoration, Cleopatra emerged as the likely heir. She would go on to marry her brothers in turn, as was customary for Ptolemaic queens, and rule as pharaoh. Egypt, unlike many other ancient societies, did not prohibit female rulers, and co-regency with male relatives became a normalized practice over the three centuries of Ptolemaic rule.

Education, Politics, and Culture

No matter what her status was in her family, Cleopatra was always bound to have a robust education, fitting for a woman of her status in the ancient world. She was born and raised in Alexandria, the intellectual center of the Hellenistic world, and had the massive Great Library at her fingertips. Though she was raised in Egypt, her family still considered themselves Greek, so Cleopatra would have had a classical Greek education. Some later sources suggest she was tutored by prominent scholars, though historians today aren't certain who they were or how reliable those claims are. Still, it's clear she had a strong foundation in literature, science, politics, and both Greek and Egyptian religion. When she was older, she might have studied with scholars affiliated with the Mouseion, a kind of scholarly academy in Alexandria, where she likely studied languages, culture, math, science, Egyptian religious practices (including her ceremonial roles), and the workings of power.

Cleopatra was known for her grasp of languages. She was a polyglot and is said to have spoken multiple languages, including Greek, Egyptian, Aramaic, at least one Persian language, and possibly others, like an Ethiopian dialect. She likely picked up some Latin too. While her reputation for speaking nine or more languages might have been exaggerated for political effect, there's no doubt that she stood out for actually learning Egyptian—something no Ptolemaic ruler had done. It was a smart political move. Being able to speak directly to her subjects without a translator would have helped her connect with them and appear more legitimate in their eyes.

She likely learned about Greek political systems during her studies, but her real education came from her life. She lived through power shifts, court intrigues, and cultural tensions. Her early life shaped her into a ruler who was clever, adaptable, and deeply aware of the mistakes her family had made—and how not to repeat them.

Ptolemy XII: The Flute Player Who Ruined Egypt

One of the last male pharaohs of Egypt was Cleopatra's father, Ptolemy XII. His reign would set the stage for everything that came after. Born around 115 BCE, Ptolemy XII came to power under a cloud of uncertain legitimacy that would haunt him his entire life, and his desperate attempts to secure his throne left Egypt politically and financially weakened.

When Ptolemy XI was lynched by an angry Alexandrian mob in 80 BCE for murdering his wife, Berenice III, he left no legitimate heir. The only surviving male descendants of Ptolemy I were the illegitimate sons of Ptolemy IX. They had been born to an unknown concubine. As the eldest, Ptolemy XII was installed as king by the Alexandrian elite.

But there was a problem. Roman sources later claimed that Ptolemy XI had left Egypt to Rome in his will, giving the Romans a pretext to assert control, though no such will has ever been found. However, the Roman Senate was divided and unwilling to take on the expense and complications of annexing Egypt, so it allowed Ptolemy XII to rule, at least for the moment. The new king knew his position was precarious. He wasn't legitimate in the traditional sense, and Rome could change its mind at any moment.

Ptolemy XII took the cult name "Neos Dionysus" ("New Dionysus"), associating himself with the god of wine, music, and divine ecstasy. This wasn't just religious devotion; the Ptolemies had long revered Dionysus, who in Greek mythology conquered Asia and was seen as a counterpart to the Egyptian god Osiris. But ancient writers mocked him mercilessly for it, giving him the derogatory nickname "Auletes" (meaning "the Flute

Player") because of his fondness for playing the aulos at musical competitions and Dionysian festivals. This was considered beneath the dignity of a king by many. It was low-class entertainment that, to his critics, made him look weak.

Buying Rome's Friendship

From the beginning, Ptolemy XII's reign was marked by one overriding obsession: securing Roman recognition of his legitimacy. He married his sister, Cleopatra V Tryphaena (in accordance with Ptolemaic tradition), and was crowned in Alexandria according to Egyptian rites in 76 BCE. But that wasn't enough. In 65 BCE, some Roman politicians raised the issue of his illegitimacy and invoked a supposed will of his predecessor, claiming that Egypt should be annexed. Ptolemy XII panicked.

His solution was simple, if ruinous: he would buy Rome's support. In 59 BCE, when Julius Caesar became consul, Ptolemy XII promised him six thousand talents—an absolutely staggering sum—in exchange for a law recognizing him as an "ally and friend of the Roman nation." Caesar passed the law, and Ptolemy XII was officially recognized. But where was an already-struggling Egypt supposed to find six thousand talents? Ptolemy XII didn't have it, so he borrowed it from Roman moneylenders at high interest rates.

To pay these debts, he raised taxes dramatically across Egypt. The burden on farmers and laborers grew unbearable. The Egyptian population, who were already resentful of their Greek rulers, grew furious. And the bribes kept coming. Ptolemy XII sent troops and money to support Pompey the Great in Palestine, paid for the upkeep of Roman forces, and continued showering Roman officials with gifts. However, when he asked for Roman military protection in return, he was repeatedly rebuffed. The Romans were happy to take his money, but they weren't about to commit legions to defend him.

The Cyprus Disaster and Exile

In 58 BCE, disaster struck. A Roman politician named Publius Clodius Pulcher proposed the annexation of Cyprus, which was still a rich Ptolemaic possession, saying that the king of Cyprus had offended Rome by failing to ransom Clodius from pirates. The pretext was enough. The Roman Republic moved to seize the island. Cato the Younger was sent to carry out the annexation. He offered Ptolemy of Cyprus, the younger brother of Ptolemy XII, a choice: abdicate and accept a comfortable retirement as a priest at the Temple of Aphrodite in Paphos or face war. Ptolemy chose suicide instead.

For many in Egypt, this was a humiliating blow. Not only had a vital Ptolemaic territory been handed over to Rome, but Ptolemy XII Auletes had failed to protect his brother or preserve the island. In 58 BCE, riots broke out in Alexandria. The Alexandrian elite and other factions declared Ptolemy XII had been deposed and proclaimed his eldest daughter, Berenice IV, as queen. (Some sources indicate she ruled jointly with Cleopatra V Tryphaena; others suggest Tryphaena was already dead.) By 57 BCE, Berenice IV stood as the sole monarch in Alexandria.

Ptolemy XII fled Egypt. He reportedly took one of his younger daughters, likely the future queen Cleopatra VII, with him. They sought refuge in Rome or some nearby allied territory. In exile, he turned to political maneuvering and bribery, hoping to win back the throne with Roman backing.

Three Years in Exile

According to later accounts, Ptolemy XII took up residence at Pompey's villa in the Alban Hills outside Rome. He lavished gifts and promises on Roman senators, cultivating allies and calling in favors. When envoys from Alexandria arrived in Rome to oppose his restoration, Ptolemy had some of them quietly eliminated.

Despite his efforts, the bribes didn't produce swift results. By late 57 BCE, the Roman Senate expressed support for his return, but when a controversial "prophecy" was presented warning against providing active military aid, the Romans hesitated. A frustrated Ptolemy departed Rome and moved to Ephesus, taking shelter in the precinct of Artemis.

Meanwhile, in Alexandria, his daughter Berenice IV staked her claim to the throne and searched for a husband to legitimize her reign. The first candidate, Seleucus, a man of obscure origins, was so despised for his vulgar manners that the Alexandrians nicknamed him "Kybiosaktes" ("the Salt-fish-monger"). Berenice had him strangled after only a few days. Eventually, she married a Cappadocian nobleman named Archelaus.

The Brutal Return

In 55 BCE, Ptolemy XII finally got what he wanted. He bribed Aulus Gabinius, the Roman proconsul of Syria, with a huge sum in return for a Roman army to invade Egypt and restore him to the throne. Gabinius, encouraged by Pompey the Great and enticed by the payment, marched into Egypt with Roman forces. Among them was a young cavalry officer named Mark Antony, who would later become important in Cleopatra's story. According to tradition, Mark Antony might have first encountered Cleopatra at this time (Cleopatra would have been about fourteen years old, while Mark Antony would have been almost thirty).

The invasion was swift. The forces of Berenice IV's consort, Archelaus, tried to resist, but his troops mutinied. Archelaus was killed, and the palace surrendered. In spring 55 BCE, Ptolemy XII was restored to the throne by Roman military might. One of his earliest acts was to eliminate his daughter Berenice IV and her supporters. She had usurped his rule, and he showed no mercy.

After being restored, Ptolemy XII ruled with the backing of roughly two thousand Roman soldiers and mercenaries (the Gabiniani), who were stationed in Alexandria. Their presence meant that Rome held effective leverage over Egypt. The debts he had incurred to pay for his restoration weighed heavily on the treasury. To meet these financial obligations, heavy taxation fell on his subjects, deepening Egypt's economic troubles. The kingdom had effectively become a client state of Rome.

The Final Years and the Co-Regency

In 52 BCE, with her father growing older, Cleopatra VII was formally made regent, a move that marked the beginning of her immersion in the business of kingship. For a time, she was being prepared to rule. She must have learned about the responsibilities she would carry as the proper ruler during that regency (though sources are scant). This hands-on learning gave her a head start when the throne passed to her.

When Ptolemy XII died in 51 BCE, his will left Egypt to Cleopatra VII and her younger brother Ptolemy XIII as joint monarchs. They were to be co-regents and spouses. However, Cleopatra, who was about eighteen, quickly became the dominant presence at court.

She inherited not only the throne but a kingdom deeply in distress. The state finances had been drained, public trust had eroded, and

Rome's influence and debt obligations loomed over Egypt. This was a fragile inheritance. Cleopatra assumed power as queen in a state that needed careful, tactful rule to survive.

The foundation of her later political skill—the alliance-building, the public-relations instincts, the delicate dance between Greek, Egyptian, and Roman interests—began in those early, turbulent years following her father's death. What she would later attempt with Roman generals, foreign diplomacy, and internal reform all had their roots in the crumbling legacy she inherited.

Chapter 3 – The Struggle for the Throne

Marriage and Co-Regency with Ptolemy XIII Philopater

As per tradition, Cleopatra and her younger brother Ptolemy XIII were designated co-rulers of Egypt after their father's death. They were likely supposed to be spouses under Ptolemaic custom, though there is no firm contemporary record that confirms their marriage. Cleopatra was about eighteen, and Ptolemy XIII was around ten. This age gap gave Cleopatra the advantage in experience, maturity, and political awareness.

Because of his youth, Ptolemy XIII was surrounded by regents and advisors who were expected to manage affairs until he came of age. These advisors soon grew wary of Cleopatra's talents and influence, particularly as she had already seen how rulership worked under her father and might have had some strong ideas about governance. Their suspicions about her loyalty and ambitions would ultimately spark a bitter rivalry that would tear the kingdom apart.

In practice, though nominally co-rulers, Cleopatra appears to have been the dominant figure. When official documents began listing her name first, it signaled that she held the actual power. Ptolemy XIII's advisors began to plot. The co-regency, which might have offered a stable transition of power, instead became a dangerous power struggle.

The Three Men Who Controlled the Boy King

To understand why Cleopatra's co-regency was doomed from the start, we need to understand the three men who controlled her brother. This wasn't just a sibling rivalry; it was a power struggle between an experienced, ambitious queen and a triumvirate of advisors who held the real power.

Pothinus (sometimes spelled Potheinous) was the most powerful of the three. A eunuch who had been appointed as Ptolemy XIII's official regent, he controlled the palace administration and Egypt's finances. Eunuchs were common in royal courts throughout the ancient world because they couldn't father children, thus posing no dynastic threat. As regent and minister, Pothinus managed Egypt's resources and debts—the key levers of political power in a kingdom drowning in obligations to Rome.

Achillas commanded Egypt's military forces, including the garrison in Alexandria and the armies stationed throughout the kingdom. Ancient sources describe him as leading substantial infantry and cavalry forces, more than enough to make him a kingmaker in times of turmoil. His appointment as one of Ptolemy's guardians gave him both military and political authority. Control of the army meant control of the kingdom, and Achillas knew this.

Theodotus of Chios was a Greek rhetorician; he was basically a professional teacher of public speaking and persuasion. He served as Ptolemy XIII's tutor. In the Hellenistic world, rhetoric was considered one of the most important skills for a ruler or statesman. As the king's tutor, Theodotus shaped not only how the young king spoke and made decisions but also how the court presented itself to Greek elites and foreign powers. His influence over Ptolemy XIII gave him considerable sway in policy decisions.

With the palace, the army, and the king's education under their control, these three men held the machinery of the state. Cleopatra had intelligence, experience from her year as co-regent, and legitimacy as the designated heir, but the triumvirate controlled the resources that could make or break a ruler in ancient Egypt.

Cleopatra understood the need to solidify her position. Early in her reign, she made public appearances, issued decrees, and worked to present herself as the rightful monarch to both Egyptians and Greeks. Although the surviving evidence for her earliest acts is limited, inscriptions and later accounts suggest she aligned herself with Egyptian religious tradition and fulfilled the ceremonial duties expected of a pharaoh. These efforts helped her cultivate support among the Egyptian populace and elites. Cleopatra knew that the goodwill of the people and the perception that she respected Egyptian customs could prove crucial in the power struggle unfolding around her.

Cleopatra vs. Ptolemy XIII

Apart from their differences in age and experience, the co-regency between Cleopatra and Ptolemy XIII was unstable from the beginning due to political and personal tensions. Cleopatra increasingly aligned herself with Rome, recognizing its growing power and the advantages of cultivating strong ties with Roman leaders. Her understanding of Roman politics was shaped in part by her father's reliance on Roman support during his reign and exile. She aimed to preserve Egypt's autonomy not by resisting Roman influence outright but by leveraging it strategically to maintain what remained of her family's rule.

In contrast, the advisors who surrounded Ptolemy XIII, particularly Pothinus, Theodotus, and Achillas, opposed Cleopatra's independent rule and likely viewed her Roman connections with suspicion. These men saw Rome's deepening involvement in Egyptian affairs as a threat to their own authority at court. They preferred the young and inexperienced Ptolemy XIII, since they could more easily manipulate him, over a politically astute queen who acted on her own initiative.

In many respects, the conflict between Cleopatra and her brother can be better understood as a power struggle between Cleopatra and the ruling council in Alexandria. These men were not accustomed to a monarch, especially not a woman, who governed with such authority and independence. Cleopatra was multilingual, politically savvy, and confident in her decision-making, which diminished the influence of the court advisors who had held sway under her father and brother. Though there had been women in power before her, including her older sister Berenice IV, the patriarchal norms of Ptolemaic society likely played a role in the council's hostility toward Cleopatra's assertive leadership.

A Kingdom in Crisis

The power struggle between Cleopatra and her brother's advisors played out against a backdrop of environmental and economic stress. Egypt was entering a period of mounting crisis, and the instability gave Pothinus and his allies a convenient opportunity to turn court opinion against the young queen.

The lifeblood of Egypt had always been the Nile's annual flood. Every summer, monsoon rains in the Ethiopian Highlands would swell the river until it overflowed its banks and flooded the surrounding plains. When the waters receded, they left behind fertile silt. But if the flood was too low, crops would fail. If it was too high, it could destroy infrastructure and livestock. The entire kingdom's survival depended on the Nile flooding at just the right level. During Cleopatra's early reign, the floods were reportedly poor.

Modern scientific research has revealed what the ancient Egyptians couldn't have known. Volcanic eruptions around the world might have disrupted the climate. When volcanoes erupt, they release sulfur dioxide into the atmosphere, forming aerosols that reflect sunlight and cool the climate. This cooling could have altered precipitation patterns, reducing the monsoon rainfall in Ethiopia that fed the Nile. Recent studies have linked major eruptions in the mid-1ˢᵗ century BCE to decreased Nile flooding, and their effects on Egypt might have been significant.

Without adequate flooding, the harvest would have suffered. Without a harvest, famine could follow. And with food in short supply, tax collection would falter. The government still needed revenue to pay back the enormous debts left by Ptolemy XII to Rome. The result could have been a vicious cycle. Crop failures put pressure on state revenues, which led to increased taxation, which in turn might have forced some rural families into debt or land sales, prompting migration into cities and fueling unrest.

Cleopatra did what she could. She couldn't control the Nile's floods, but she reportedly took steps to stabilize the countryside, perhaps by issuing guidance on irrigation or working to check the abuses of local officials. However, the crisis was likely too large for any one ruler to manage, especially a young queen still consolidating her power.

Pothinus saw his opportunity. It was easy to pin Egypt's troubles on Cleopatra. She was young, female, and making decisions independently without deferring to the "experienced" council. In Egyptian tradition, the pharaoh was expected to uphold ma'at (cosmic order and balance). If the Nile failed to flood properly, some might have interpreted it as a sign of divine displeasure. Whether through religious undertones or court politics, Pothinus and his allies began to circulate the idea that Cleopatra's assertiveness and her failure to share power with her brother, as their father's will had outlined, had brought misfortune to the kingdom.

By 49 BCE, after several years of instability and hardship, Cleopatra's position had weakened. Though the environmental crisis was not her fault, it became a weapon in the political battle that drove her from power.

During the first few years of her reign, Pothinus and his followers continued to resist Cleopatra's growing independence and diplomatic overtures to Rome. By 48 BCE, they had gained the upper hand in Ptolemy XIII's name. With military backing and control of Alexandria, they forced Cleopatra to flee the capital. This exile tested her resilience and political instincts, but it ultimately proved to be a turning point in her campaign to restore her authority.

Exile from Alexandria

Cleopatra was only about nineteen or twenty years old when she found herself ousted from the place she called home. Ptolemy XIII's advisors, led by Potheinous, succeeded in forcing her from power, and she fled Egypt for Syria.

In 49 BCE, Syria was under Roman influence, which offered Cleopatra a degree of safety from her brother's forces. While this was her first exile, she had witnessed political turmoil during her father's reign and understood the power of Roman backing.

In Syria, Cleopatra began to gather support for her return. Though ancient sources don't detail her alliances in the region, she likely tried to revive political networks first built during her father's reign. However, the Roman world she inherited had changed.

While the extent of local support is unclear, Cleopatra began to raise a force to reclaim the throne. She also had her younger sister Arsinoe IV with her, which might have added legitimacy to her claim, presenting her not as a lone exile but as a contender representing another branch of the royal family.

Building an Army

The key to Cleopatra's return was military force. Ptolemy XIII controlled Alexandria and commanded the Egyptian army under Achillas, so Cleopatra needed to raise her own. Ancient sources tell us only that she assembled a force during her exile, likely drawing on the wide networks of mercenaries active throughout the eastern Mediterranean. This region was home to many professional soldiers—Greeks, Thracians, Arabs, and others displaced by the constant wars between Hellenistic states. These men hired themselves out to whoever could offer to pay them and had a plausible chance of victory.

Cleopatra might have carried some money with her when she fled Egypt, but more importantly, she had royal legitimacy. Her claim to the throne had been endorsed by her father's will and, originally, by Rome. That credibility could have made her an appealing patron to mercenaries and regional leaders who stood to benefit if she regained power.

Some later sources suggest she might have sought support from neighboring Arab groups, possibly Nabataean or other tribal forces from the east or south of Judea. These would not have been large professional armies but smaller contingents tied to local rulers who might have seen political advantages in backing Cleopatra's return.

The Return to Egypt

By the spring of 48 BCE, Cleopatra had gathered enough forces to make her move. But she was strategic about it. She didn't march directly on Alexandria; that would likely have been disastrous. Ptolemy XIII controlled the capital and had the Egyptian army, including a sizable force of infantry and cavalry, under his control through Achillas. Instead, Cleopatra positioned her forces at Pelusium, the fortress city on Egypt's northeastern frontier. This was a calculated move for several reasons.

First, Pelusium controlled the main land route into Egypt from the east. By holding it, Cleopatra could secure her entry point and shield herself from immediate retaliation while she remained outside the heart of the kingdom. Second, it placed her close enough to Egyptian territory to assert her claim to the throne but not so deep inside the country that she risked being surrounded or cut off if her campaign failed. Third, Pelusium was where many arrivals from the eastern Mediterranean, possibly even fleeing Romans, would have landed when entering Egypt.

She couldn't have known it at the time, but this positioning would soon become significant. Within months, the Roman civil war between Caesar and Pompey would reach Egyptian shores, and Cleopatra's presence at Pelusium placed her near the epicenter of what followed. For the moment, though, she and her brother were in a tense standoff. These two rival factions were confronting one another along the eastern edge of Egypt, neither able to decisively defeat the other.

Cleopatra had clawed her way back from exile to the gates of her homeland. She had raised an army, cultivated key alliances, and positioned herself with care. However, she still lacked the power to unseat her brother and reclaim her throne. For that, she would need support from Rome—and that support was about to arrive in the form of Julius Caesar.

A sculpture of Julius Caesar. [2]

Chapter 4 – Alliance with Caesar

Caesar's Arrival in Egypt

While Cleopatra and Ptolemy XIII were locked in a stalemate on Egypt's frontier, the Roman Republic was tearing itself apart in a civil war. Julius Caesar and Pompey the Great—once allies in Rome's First Triumvirate—had become bitter enemies, each vying for control of Rome. After Caesar defied the Senate and crossed the Rubicon in 49 BCE, the two generals clashed across the Mediterranean. Though Caesar's forces were smaller, his bold strategy and loyal legions delivered a series of victories that ultimately forced Pompey to flee.

In September 48 BCE, after his crushing defeat at the Battle of Pharsalus, Pompey arrived at Pelusium seeking refuge. He had enjoyed close ties with Ptolemy XII, had played a role in ratifying the late king's will, and likely believed that Egypt, which was now under the rule of his son, Ptolemy XIII, would offer sanctuary. It was a fatal miscalculation.

Pothinus, Achillas, and Theodotus faced a difficult choice. To shelter Pompey risked Caesar's wrath. To reject him invited danger from a desperate and cornered general. According to ancient accounts, Theodotus argued that neither course was safe—only assassination would remove the threat. On September 28th, 48 BCE, as Pompey's boat approached the shore, Achillas and a Roman officer named Lucius Septimius rowed out to meet him. They murdered him in the boat and severed his head.

Two days later, Caesar arrived in Alexandria with a fairly small force. Pothinus and his allies presented him with Pompey's head and signet ring, expecting gratitude. Instead, Caesar responded with revulsion. According to some sources, he wept. However, Caesar's reaction was not just sentimental; it was also political. He had built his image on mercy toward defeated enemies, a strategy that had earned him a lot of support in Rome. Pompey's murder had robbed him of the chance to offer forgiveness publicly, and it ensured that Pompey's sons would continue the war rather than accept defeat.

The assassination had backfired. If anything, it pushed Caesar closer to Cleopatra's camp and set the stage for a new chapter in the power struggle for Egypt.

The Carpet Meeting

Recognizing the opportunity of Caesar's presence, Cleopatra made her boldest move yet. Caesar was staying in the royal palace in Alexandria as an honored guest of Ptolemy XIII. Cleopatra couldn't simply walk through the palace gates. Achillas controlled the city, and she risked arrest or death if discovered. She needed to reach Caesar without being detected.

The story of what happened next comes from Plutarch, who wrote more than a century later. According to his account, Cleopatra enlisted the services of a Sicilian merchant named Apollodorus. She climbed into a large sack, likely a bedding sack used for linens. Apollodorus tied it up and carried it through the palace. Once inside Caesar's private chambers, he unrolled the sack, and Cleopatra emerged.

The popular image of a "carpet" likely stems from a later mistranslation. Plutarch's original Greek describes a bedding sack or linen bag, but 18th-century translators, such as John Langhorne, rendered it as a "carpet," possibly due to a lack of an exact English equivalent or for dramatic flair. The carpet version stuck and was immortalized in paintings and films. But whether it was a sack or a rug, the core truth remains: Cleopatra smuggled herself into Caesar's chambers in a dramatic, risky gambit.

According to Plutarch, Caesar was immediately captivated by her boldness and charm. We don't know what they discussed that night, but we know the outcome. Caesar soon threw his support behind Cleopatra. The next day, he summoned both siblings and announced that they would rule together as co-regents, just as their father's will had specified.

But everyone understood that Caesar was backing Cleopatra.

For Cleopatra, this was everything. Caesar commanded battle-hardened Roman legions. His endorsement gave her legitimacy in the eyes of Rome and the Alexandrian elite. For Caesar, the alliance made sense too. Cleopatra was intelligent, experienced, and politically astute. She would be a reliable ally who could keep Egypt's grain flowing to Rome. Ptolemy XIII's faction, by contrast, had just demonstrated its instability and short-sightedness by murdering Pompey.

The Alexandrian War

Pothinus and Achillas were outraged. They hadn't assassinated Pompey and controlled Egypt for months just to hand power back to Cleopatra on Caesar's say-so. They began plotting immediately.

Caesar had only about 3,200 soldiers with him—a tiny force by military standards. Achillas commanded the Egyptian army, which some modern estimates suggest might have numbered around twenty thousand men, though this figure is not confirmed in ancient sources. Either way, the Egyptians vastly outnumbered the Romans. In late 48 BCE, Achillas brought his forces into Alexandria and launched an attack on the royal quarter where Caesar was staying with his soldiers and the Ptolemaic royal family.

What followed was urban warfare in one of the ancient world's greatest cities. Caesar managed to hold the royal palace and the harbor, giving him access to the sea and potential reinforcements. His troops fought the Egyptians in Alexandria's streets and in naval skirmishes in the harbor.

The Battle for the Harbor

One of Caesar's first priorities was securing his naval position. Much of the Egyptian fleet was docked in the harbor when the siege began, possibly undergoing routine maintenance, with crews likely dispersed throughout the city. Caesar moved quickly, sending his men to burn the Egyptian ships before they could be used against him. The fires spread. According to some ancient sources, the fires reached part of the famous Library of Alexandria, though the extent of the damage remains debated by historians.

The Egyptians weren't finished. They managed to preserve a portion of their naval force and continued to outfit additional ships. The Egyptian forces launched a particularly cunning attack. They cut off the freshwater supply to the Roman-held section of the city. Caesar's soldiers were close to panic until he ordered them to dig wells, which successfully found fresh water beneath the city.

The Fight for Pharos Island

Caesar understood that controlling Alexandria's harbor meant controlling the island of Pharos, home to the famous lighthouse and one of the Seven Wonders of the Ancient World. The lighthouse wasn't just a marvel of engineering. It also stood on a fortified island that commanded the entrance to the harbor. If Caesar could hold Pharos, the Egyptians couldn't blockade him.

He led an amphibious assault on the island, landing troops from small boats while his fleet provided covering fire. The fighting was fierce. The island was defended by a Ptolemaic garrison and possibly some local inhabitants. Eventually, Caesar's troops forced the defenders to retreat into the town on Pharos, and the Romans captured most of the island.

However, holding it proved harder than taking it. The island was connected to the mainland by the Heptastadion—a causeway about three-quarters of a mile long, with channels or passages at key points. Caesar needed to control this causeway to prevent the Egyptians from attacking his positions. The next day, he landed more troops and began fortifying his position on the causeway.

The Egyptians launched a sudden two-pronged counterattack by land and sea. Caesar's light infantry, caught between the Egyptian assault from the mainland and enemy ships attacking from the water, was quickly overwhelmed by the better-armed Ptolemaic soldiers. In the chaos, Caesar's men began a panicked retreat to their boats.

Caesar himself was caught in the melee. His small ship was swamped by fleeing soldiers trying to escape, and it began to sink. According to Plutarch, Caesar, wearing his distinctive purple cloak that made him an easy target, threw himself into the water. He swam about two hundred paces to safety, reportedly holding important documents above the water with one hand while swimming with the other. Some sources say he dragged his purple cloak through the water with his teeth to prevent the Egyptians from capturing it as a trophy.

The battle ended in defeat. Caesar lost control of the causeway and suffered about four hundred legionaries killed. Another four hundred sailors drowned, according to later sources. It was one of his rare setbacks, though he maintained control of most of Pharos Island itself.

The Siege Drags On

During the fighting, Caesar had Pothinus executed. Ancient sources say he discovered the eunuch was sending messages to Achillas and possibly conspiring with the Egyptian forces. Some later accounts suggest he might have tried to poison Cleopatra. His death created a power vacuum in the Egyptian command structure that Cleopatra's younger sister would attempt to fill.

Arsinoe IV, who was probably around fifteen or sixteen years old at the time, had been held with her siblings in the palace when the siege began. At some point early in the conflict, she managed to escape from Caesar's custody and made her way to the Egyptian forces besieging the palace. The army proclaimed her queen, making this a three-way civil war. Now Cleopatra (with Caesar), Ptolemy XIII (nominally in Caesar's custody but still a figurehead for the loyalists), and Arsinoe were all claiming the throne.

Arsinoe brought her chief advisor, a eunuch named Ganymedes, with her to the Egyptian camp. Almost immediately, she and General Achillas began quarreling over who should command the army. The power struggle ended when Arsinoe had Achillas assassinated. Ganymedes took over military command of the Egyptian forces. Under Ganymedes's leadership, the Egyptians launched some of their most effective attacks, including the cunning scheme to cut off the freshwater supply to Caesar's forces that nearly caused panic among the Roman soldiers.

For months, the siege continued, with Arsinoe and Ganymedes leading the Egyptian forces. Caesar was trapped in the palace quarter with dwindling supplies and no way to break out. The Egyptians couldn't dislodge him, but he also couldn't advance. Both sides settled into a stalemate. There was street fighting, occasional naval skirmishes, and artillery exchanges. Alexandria's citizens were caught in the middle, their city becoming a battlefield.

Interestingly, a delegation of Alexandrians eventually approached Caesar, asking him to release Ptolemy XIII. They claimed they were tired of being ruled by Arsinoe and Ganymedes. Whether this represented genuine popular sentiment or was orchestrated by Ptolemy's remaining supporters is unclear. Caesar agreed, apparently calculating that releasing the boy might divide his enemies. It didn't work as planned. Ptolemy XIII immediately took command of the Egyptian forces from Arsinoe and renewed the attacks with fresh determination. What happened to Arsinoe at this point is unclear. She seems to have been sidelined when her brother took over, but she remained with the Egyptian forces.

The Relief and Final Victory

Finally, in early 47 BCE, Roman reinforcements arrived from the east under Mithridates of Pergamum. He brought a mixed force of Roman troops and allied soldiers, including a Jewish contingent contributed by High Priest Hyrcanus II, which was led by Antipater; later sources say it numbered around three thousand men. Mithridates stormed the fortress city of Pelusium on Egypt's eastern frontier and then began marching toward Alexandria.

Ptolemy XIII took much of his army out of Alexandria to intercept Mithridates before he could link up with Caesar. Caesar, seeing his chance, broke out of the city with his troops and marched to join forces with Mithridates. The two armies met somewhere in the Nile Delta region.

In the decisive Battle of the Nile, in late January or early February 47 BCE, Caesar's combined forces crushed the Egyptian army. The battle was a rout. Ptolemy XIII fled the battlefield and attempted to escape by boat across the Nile, but in the chaos, his vessel was reportedly overloaded with panicked soldiers. It capsized and sank. The fifteen-year-old king drowned, weighed down by his armor. His body was later recovered from the river.

With Ptolemy XIII dead and Arsinoe captured, the war was over. Caesar marched back to Alexandria, and the city surrendered without further resistance. Arsinoe was taken prisoner, and she would later be paraded in Caesar's triumph in Rome before being exiled to the Temple of Artemis at Ephesus.

With her rivals defeated, Cleopatra was installed as the sole ruler of Egypt. To maintain the appearance of traditional Ptolemaic co-regency, she married her youngest brother, the twelve-year-old Ptolemy XIV, and made him her nominal co-regent. However, everyone understood he ruled in name only. Cleopatra was the undisputed queen of Egypt, and she had Caesar to thank for it.

Caesar Lingers in Egypt

The Roman civil war wasn't over. Pompey's sons were still fighting in North Africa and Spain. Caesar's presence was urgently needed back in Rome, where his absence had created political chaos. Yet Caesar didn't leave Egypt immediately after his victory.

Modern scholars believe he stayed for approximately two to three months, roughly from late January or early February until April or May of 47 BCE. Ancient sources offer various explanations. Perhaps he was resting after the exhausting siege, waiting for favorable sailing winds, or simply enjoying his time with Cleopatra. The truth was likely a combination of political necessity, practical concerns, and personal desire.

The relationship between Cleopatra and Caesar was both political and personal, though where one ended and the other began is impossible to say. Their partnership was built on mutual necessity and mutual benefit, but ancient sources also make it clear that genuine affection developed between them. They were well matched intellectually; both were brilliant, ambitious, and politically astute. Ancient writers describe how they would talk late into the night and how Caesar was fascinated by her intelligence and charm.

Politically, Caesar needed to ensure Cleopatra's regime was stable. He couldn't afford to have Egypt descend into another civil war the moment he left. He left behind three Roman legions—about fifteen thousand soldiers—to garrison Egypt and protect the new queen. This was a substantial force that demonstrated Rome's commitment to Cleopatra's rule while ensuring Egypt would remain under Roman influence. He also returned the island of Cyprus to Egyptian control, a gesture that helped legitimize Cleopatra's rule in the eyes of her subjects. Cyprus had been annexed by Rome years earlier under her father's troubled reign.

For Cleopatra, Caesar's support was everything. His military power had secured her throne. His endorsement gave her legitimacy in the eyes of both Egyptians and the wider Mediterranean world. His protection meant that no one—not rival Ptolemies, not ambitious courtiers, not foreign enemies—would dare challenge her while Caesar lived. Egypt needed Rome's backing to survive, and Caesar was Rome's most powerful man.

For Caesar, the alliance made equal sense. Egypt was the wealthiest kingdom in the Mediterranean, and its grain exports were critical for feeding Rome's population. By backing Cleopatra, he secured a reliable, grateful ally who would ensure that grain kept flowing to Rome at stable prices. He also gained access to Egypt's vast wealth without having to spend the time, money, and manpower to conquer it. A friendly Egypt was far more valuable than a hostile one.

There were also practical matters to attend to. Caesar made plans for construction projects in Alexandria, including a monument to himself that would later be called the Caesareum. Though he wouldn't have time to complete it, Cleopatra would take on the project after his departure. He likely spent time meeting with scholars at Alexandria's famous library and museum, discussing mathematics, astronomy, and geography.

In the spring of 47 BCE, Caesar joined Cleopatra on a lavish cruise up the Nile. The stated purpose was to show the Egyptian people their queen, to visit temples, and to reinforce Cleopatra's connection with Egyptian religion and tradition. Cleopatra styled herself as the living incarnation of Isis, the Egyptian goddess of fertility, motherhood, and protection.

There was no strategic reason for Caesar to join this cruise. He had urgent business in Rome. Yet he stayed, traveling with Cleopatra on her opulent royal barge. Ancient sources describe the vessel as spectacular. It was like a floating palace with dining halls, gardens, and elaborate decorations. Each night brought lavish banquets. The cruise allowed Caesar to see Egypt's wealth firsthand—its ancient monuments, its fertile farmland, and its resources. But more than that, it was an extended interlude of luxury and romance, far from the battlefields and political games.

Eventually, duty called Caesar away. In mid-47 BCE, he left Egypt to deal with a rebellion in Anatolia (where he would famously declare "Veni, vidi, vici"—"I came, I saw, I conquered"). A few months after his departure, Cleopatra gave birth to a son. She named him Ptolemy XV Philopator Philometor Caesar, but he was known to history by his nickname, "Caesarion," or "Little Caesar."

Though Caesar never formally acknowledged Caesarion as his son, he never denied it either, and he treated the boy with affection during Cleopatra's later visit to Rome. For Cleopatra, Caesarion represented a potential dynasty, a link between Egypt's throne and Rome's power.

Cleopatra in Rome

In 46 BCE, Cleopatra traveled to Rome with her co-ruler, the young Ptolemy XIV, and possibly her son, Caesarion. She stayed in Caesar's villa across the Tiber River, which was a very public statement of their relationship.

She came to strengthen Egypt's alliance with Rome, to gain formal recognition from the Senate, and to pursue her long-term goal of recovering Egyptian territories lost by previous Ptolemaic rulers. Her lavish entourage made a powerful impression, reminding Romans that Egypt was wealthy and sophisticated, not just another conquered province.

Personally, she came to be with Caesar and, perhaps, to have him acknowledge their son. Caesar commissioned a golden statue of her in the Temple of Venus Genetrix, reportedly depicted in the guise of Isis-Venus. This sparked a cultural fascination with Egypt among Rome's elite—the latest outbreak of what we now call "Egyptomania." Egyptian motifs appeared in Roman art and architecture. Egyptian fashion influenced Roman dress. The worship of Isis and Serapis spread through Rome.

But not everyone was enchanted. The orator Cicero described Cleopatra with contempt in his letters, calling her arrogant and detailing his disdain for her. Many Romans were scandalized by Caesar's relationship with a foreign queen and his treatment of Caesarion. Some feared Cleopatra's influence over Caesar was leading him toward creating a monarchy, a concept that Romans despised.

The most lasting contribution often associated with Cleopatra's Roman visit was the Julian calendar. The Egyptian solar calendar of 365 days had been in use for millennia and was far more accurate than Rome's confusing lunisolar calendar. Caesar, impressed by its precision, reformed the Roman calendar. He consulted the Alexandrian astronomer Sosigenes to work out the details. The resulting Julian Calendar—365 days divided into 12 months, with a leap year every fourth year—became the standard in the Western world for over 1,600 years.

The Ides of March

On March 15th, 44 BCE, Julius Caesar was assassinated. A group of senators, led by Brutus and Cassius, stabbed him to death during a Senate meeting. They called themselves the Liberators and claimed they were saving the Roman Republic from tyranny. Earlier that year, Caesar had been appointed dictator for life, and the conspirators feared he intended to make himself king.

Cleopatra was in Rome when it happened. Ancient sources don't record her immediate reaction, but given what followed, one can infer that she was shocked and shifted into survival mode. She remained in Rome for a few weeks, apparently hoping to have Caesarion acknowledged as Caesar's heir. However, Caesar's will named only his grand-nephew Gaius Octavius (better known as Octavian and later known as Augustus) as his heir. Caesarion was not officially mentioned.

Realizing that Caesarion would likely gain no recognition under Roman law, Cleopatra spent her remaining time in Rome gathering information. She understood that whoever emerged victorious in the coming power struggle would determine Egypt's fate. Then she returned to Alexandria.

Caesar's assassination threw much of the Mediterranean into chaos. However, Cleopatra had, to a degree, prepared for the storm. She still had the throne, her son, and Egypt's wealth. What she lacked, however, was the patronage of Rome's master. The next great Roman to enter her life would be Mark Antony, and with him came new opportunities and troubles.

Chapter 5 –
Mark Antony and the End

Cleopatra's Return to Egypt

One month after Caesar's assassination in March 44 BCE, Cleopatra returned to Alexandria with her son Caesarion. The journey back must have been filled with uncertainty. Caesar was dead. Rome was descending into chaos. And Cleopatra had just spent months in the heart of the Roman Republic, openly living as Caesar's mistress, trying unsuccessfully to have their son recognized as his heir. Now she had to return to Egypt and figure out how to survive what came next.

Her first priority was consolidating power at home. During her absence in Rome, Egypt had been overseen by her younger brother and co-ruler, Ptolemy XIV, along with advisors loyal to Cleopatra. But Cleopatra had learned her lesson from the disasters with Ptolemy XIII and his advisors. She wasn't going to let another ambitious brother or his counselors threaten her throne.

Shortly after her return, Ptolemy XIV died under what ancient sources call "mysterious circumstances." He was about fifteen years old. No ancient writer directly accuses Cleopatra of poisoning him, but the timing was awfully convenient, and few modern historians doubt she was responsible. She immediately made the three-year-old Caesarion her new co-ruler, giving him the throne name Ptolemy XV Caesar. Cleopatra was now the undisputed ruler of Egypt, with complete control over her kingdom.

She could see the chaos spreading through the Roman world, and she didn't want a repeat of the Alexandrian War happening while Rome tore itself apart. Her goal was to stabilize Egypt, maintain economic production, and position herself to influence whichever Roman faction eventually won. With Egypt's vast wealth and grain exports, she had the resources to back a winner when the time came to choose.

For now, she would wait and watch from Alexandria while Rome burned.

Rome's Power Struggle

Caesar had died without a clear succession plan, creating a power vacuum that threatened to tear the Roman Republic apart. Multiple factions emerged, each claiming to be Caesar's true heir or defender of the republic. The assassins—Brutus, Cassius, and their allies—controlled armies in the East. Caesar's supporters rallied around different leaders. It was the kind of chaos that could easily spill into Egypt if Cleopatra wasn't careful.

By the end of 43 BCE, three men had emerged as the dominant powers: Mark Antony, Caesar's longtime friend and consul; Octavian, Caesar's adopted son and designated heir; and Lepidus, a capable general and statesman. They formed what is known as the Second Triumvirate. This power-sharing agreement would allow the men to rule Rome together and avenge Caesar's death.

Of course, these weren't the only players. Cassius, one of Caesar's assassins, built up considerable power in Syria and posed an ongoing threat. Some later accounts suggest he or his supporters approached Cleopatra for aid. She reportedly declined, citing Egypt's internal instability (economic troubles and uncertain Nile floods). Instead, she is said to have quietly backed a loyalist of Caesar (Dolabella), sending support to him in hopes of aligning with the eventual victor. Unfortunately for her, those efforts didn't lead to much. The reinforcements sent under Egypt's backing were intercepted, and her own governor in Cyprus is alleged to have defected to Cassius's side.

In October 42 BCE, the showdown came at the Battle of Philippi in Greece, where the forces of Brutus and Cassius confronted the armies of Antony and Octavian. The Triumvirate won decisively. Both conspirators committed suicide rather than face capture. Caesar had, in effect, been avenged.

After the victory, Octavian, who had recently recovered from illness during the campaign, returned to Rome to consolidate control over the west. Antony, the more experienced general, remained in the East. He toured Greece and Asia Minor, reorganized the eastern provinces, and began preparations for future campaigns. Among his first moves was to summon Cleopatra. Their union would shape the fate of both Egypt and Rome.

Who Was Mark Antony?

Marcus Antonius (better known as Mark Antony) was born around 83 BCE into a prominent but financially troubled Roman family. He was distantly related to Caesar through his mother's side. His early years were marked by a reputation for reckless behavior, including gambling debts, heavy drinking, and affairs. It was the kind of hedonism that scandalized Rome's conservative elite but made him popular with soldiers and common Romans.

A denarius depicting Mark Antony.'

However, Antony wasn't just a playboy. He was also a brilliant military commander and a charismatic politician. He'd cut his teeth in the military under Aulus Gabinius (yes, the same Gabinius who had restored Ptolemy XII to the Egyptian throne), serving in campaigns in Judea and Egypt. He later joined Caesar's staff and became one of his most trusted commanders, serving with distinction in the conquest of Gaul and during the civil war against Pompey.

Antony had probably encountered Cleopatra briefly during her time in Rome with Caesar, but there's no evidence they had any significant interaction. At that time, Antony was married to a politically active, ambitious woman named Fulvia. She would later lead a rebellion on his behalf. He was known for his oratory skills and his ability to work a crowd. His funeral speech after Caesar's assassination had turned public opinion against the conspirators so effectively that they'd been driven from Rome by an angry mob.

Physically, Antony cut an impressive figure. Ancient sources describe him as tall and strong, with a style that reportedly evoked Hercules. He apparently liked to wear his toga draped like the hero's lion skin. He cultivated a connection to Dionysus (the Greek Bacchus), the god of wine and revelry, which fit his personality perfectly. He was passionate, impulsive, loyal to his friends, and dangerous to his enemies.

He was also everything Caesar had not been. Mark Antony was emotional where Caesar was calculating, impulsive where Caesar was strategic, and oriented toward pleasure where Caesar had been oriented toward power. These differences would matter greatly in the years to come.

The Summons to Tarsus

In 41 BCE, Antony sent messages to Cleopatra demanding she come to Tarsus in Cilicia (southern Turkey) to answer charges. He claimed she had supported Cassius in the recent civil war by providing aid to Caesar's murderers. This was likely exaggerated. Her governor in Cyprus had defected and aided Cassius, but that wasn't necessarily Cleopatra's doing. Her actual support appears to have gone to the Caesarian faction.

The real reason for the summons was likely strategic. Antony needed money and resources for his planned Parthian campaign. Egypt was the wealthiest kingdom in the region, and Cleopatra controlled that wealth. He wanted to assess her loyalty and secure her support. He also wanted to remind her that Rome—specifically, he—held power over Egypt's fate.

Cleopatra didn't rush to comply, though. She received several summons, both from Antony and from his friends, but she delayed. Some sources suggest she was annoyed by the tone of his messages. Others suggest she was being strategic, making him wait while she prepared her entrance. Either way, when she finally decided to come, she made sure it would be memorable.

The Meeting on the Cydnus

Plutarch, writing about a century later, describes the scene in vivid detail that has captivated imaginations ever since. Cleopatra sailed up the River Cydnus (now known as the Berdan River) toward Tarsus in a barge fit for a goddess. The stern was gilded, the sails were made of purple silk, and silver oars kept time to the music of flutes, pipes, and lutes. She reclined beneath a canopy of gold cloth, dressed and posed as Venus (Aphrodite). Beautiful attendants dressed as sea nymphs and the Graces stood at the rudders and ropes. The air was filled with incredible perfumes and burning incense.

It was theater, and it was brilliant. Cleopatra had done her research. Antony styled himself as the new Dionysus, the god of wine and ecstasy. Cleopatra presented herself as Aphrodite, the goddess of love and beauty. She was appealing to his vanity and his love of Greek culture. And it worked.

Antony invited her to dinner. She declined and invited him to dine with her instead, immediately establishing who held the upper hand. When Antony arrived at her ship, he found a luxurious feast. The entire vessel was decorated with thousands of lamps arranged in geometric patterns. The food and wine were exquisite. The entertainment was spectacular.

Ancient sources preserve a story about their second dinner. Antony boasted that he could provide the finest banquet in the world. Cleopatra bet him she could spend ten million sesterces (an enormous sum) on a single meal. The next night, she served a fine but not exceptional banquet. Antony mocked her, saying she had lost the bet. At the end of the meal, Cleopatra called for a cup of vinegar. She removed one of her enormous pearl earrings—pearls worth millions—dropped it in the vinegar, waited for it to dissolve, and drank it. Before she could dissolve the second pearl, the judge declared her the winner.

Whether this actually happened or is a later embellishment doesn't really matter. What matters is that it captured how contemporaries and later Roman authors saw their relationship. Cleopatra was an exotic, wealthy, powerful queen who could astonish even Rome's most worldly general.

Antony was smitten. He postponed his Parthian campaign and returned with her to Alexandria.

The Inimitable Livers

Back in Alexandria, Cleopatra and Antony created what they called the "Society of the Inimitable Livers." It was essentially a private club devoted to luxury, pleasure, and living life to its fullest. They hosted elaborate banquets, gambling parties, hunting expeditions, and drinking contests. According to ancient sources, they even roamed the streets at night in disguise, playing pranks on citizens. It was hedonistic, it was excessive, and it was exactly the kind of thing Antony relished.

But it wasn't all pleasure. Cleopatra was also working to secure Antony's support, demonstrate Egypt's wealth and value as an ally, and position herself for whatever came next in Rome's shifting power struggles. She understood that Antony's alliance was crucial for Egypt's survival. Rome was the dominant power in the Mediterranean, and only a strong Roman patron could preserve Egypt's autonomy.

In 41 BCE, during this period in Alexandria, Cleopatra made sure to eliminate a lingering threat.

The Execution of Arsinoe

Arsinoe IV had been living in exile at the Temple of Artemis in Ephesus since Caesar had paraded her in his triumph in 46 BCE. The temple was a sanctuary. Ancient tradition held that anyone seeking asylum there was under the goddess's protection. For five years, Arsinoe had lived there under that protection, although she remained a potential rival to Cleopatra's throne.

She was dangerous because she was legitimate. As another daughter of Ptolemy XII, she had as much claim to Egypt's throne as Cleopatra did. She had already been proclaimed queen once during the Alexandrian War. As long as she lived, she could be a rallying point for anyone who wanted to challenge Cleopatra. If Cleopatra died, Arsinoe might try to claim the throne. If Cleopatra's enemies wanted a puppet ruler for Egypt, Arsinoe was made for the role.

Cleopatra asked Antony to deal with it, and Antony complied. He sent orders to Ephesus to execute Arsinoe.

The assassination was shocking since it violated the sacred sanctuary. Soldiers entered the Temple of Artemis—one of the Seven Wonders of the Ancient World and one of the most sacred sites in the ancient world—and dragged Arsinoe out. They killed her on the steps of the temple, likely in late 41 BCE. She was in her early twenties.

The killing outraged many. Violating the temple sanctuary was considered sacrilege. It also showed the lengths to which Cleopatra and Antony would go to eliminate threats. It damaged Cleopatra's reputation; even those who understood the political necessity found the method distasteful. But from Cleopatra's perspective, it was worth it. Arsinoe was gone. There were no more rival Ptolemies (except her young son Caesarion, who posed no threat). The throne was secure.

This was the darker side of Cleopatra's rule. She had likely poisoned Ptolemy XIV. Arsinoe was assassinated in a sacred temple. These aren't the actions of a romantic heroine of legend. They were the actions of a ruthless ruler doing what she believed necessary to survive in a brutal political landscape.

The Roman Republic in green and Ptolemaic Egypt in yellow.*

A Romance Interrupted

Antony and Cleopatra's idyllic winter in Alexandria couldn't last. In early 40 BCE, news reached them that the situation in Italy had deteriorated. Antony's wife, Fulvia, and his brother, Lucius, had been campaigning on his behalf against Octavian, and tensions had exploded into open conflict. They had raised an army and rebelled against Octavian's authority in what became known as the Perusine War.

The Parthians had also invaded Roman territory in Syria, taking advantage of Antony's absence and the chaos in Rome. Antony had to leave Egypt. He sailed for Greece and then to Italy.

By the time he reached Brundisium (modern Brindisi, Italy) in the summer of 40 BCE, the situation had changed dramatically. Octavian's forces had crushed the rebellion. Fulvia was dead. Ancient sources say she died of illness, though the timing was awfully convenient. Whether her death was natural or not, it removed a major complication from Antony's life.

At Brundisium, Antony and Octavian nearly went to war with each other. Antony's soldiers refused to let his ships into the harbor. Both sides assembled armies. Civil war seemed imminent. However, cooler heads prevailed. Neither side was ready for all-out conflict. Instead, they negotiated.

The Treaty of Brundisium redivided the Roman world. Octavian would control the west (Italy, Gaul, and Spain). Antony would control the East (Greece, Asia Minor, Syria, and Egypt). Lepidus, who had been increasingly sidelined, got North Africa. To seal the alliance, Antony—now conveniently a widower—married Octavian's sister, Octavia.

Octavia was everything a Roman wife was supposed to be. She was virtuous, dignified, politically astute, and loyal to her family. The marriage was a political arrangement, but by all accounts, Antony treated her with respect and even affection. For three years, they lived together in Athens. She bore him two daughters, Antonia Major and Antonia Minor (the latter would be the mother of Emperor Claudius).

But Antony never forgot Cleopatra. And Egypt's wealth would prove essential for his ambitions in the East.

Return to the East

For three years (40–37 BCE), Antony governed the eastern provinces with Octavia as his wife, but his mind was on Parthia. The Parthian Empire (roughly modern-day Iran and Iraq) controlled lucrative eastern trade routes and had long challenged Roman power in the East. Back in 53 BCE, Crassus, the third member of Caesar's First Triumvirate, had been killed leading an army against Parthia, and his legionary standards had been captured—a humiliation that still stung Roman pride.

A successful Parthian campaign could transform Antony's fortunes. It would bring glory, wealth from conquests, and the kind of military prestige that could rival Octavian's growing influence in Rome. It might even allow Antony to avenge Crassus's defeat and reclaim the lost standards. However, launching such a campaign would require massive resources, including soldiers, supplies, money, and logistical support.

This meant Antony needed Cleopatra.

The Meeting at Antioch

In 37 BCE, Antony summoned Cleopatra to meet him at Antioch in Syria. This time, there was no pretense of legal charges. He needed her support for the Parthian campaign, and he was willing to pay for it.

Cleopatra came, and she came with demands. She'd spent three years ruling Egypt, watching Antony's marriage to Octavia and waiting for her opportunity. Now she had leverage, and she intended to use it. Her goal had always been to restore Egypt's former glory. She wanted to recover the territories that earlier Ptolemies had lost to Rome and other powers.

The resulting agreement was unprecedented. In exchange for Egypt's financial support and grain supplies for his army, Antony granted Cleopatra rights over substantial territories, such as parts of Phoenicia (coastal Lebanon), Coele-Syria, Cyprus, and parts of Cilicia (southern Turkey). These were Roman-controlled regions, not Antony's personal property to distribute. No Roman leader had ever extended such authority to a foreign ruler in this way.

The deal angered local rulers whose territories were affected, especially Herod of Judea, who already had a bitter rivalry with Cleopatra and now lost some coastal cities to her influence. It also provided ammunition for Octavian's propaganda machine back in Rome: Antony was giving away Roman conquests to his foreign lover.

But for Cleopatra, it was a triumph. With these territorial grants, Egypt's power and wealth increased dramatically. The eastern Mediterranean seacoast gave her access to valuable timber (Egypt had no trees suitable for shipbuilding), ports, and trade routes. It was the closest she had come to restoring the Ptolemaic Empire's former extent, even if her authority over these regions was more political than administrative.

Antony also formally recognized the twins Cleopatra had borne—Alexander Helios and Cleopatra Selene, now about six years old—as his children. He had apparently known about them since their birth in 40

BCE, but formal recognition was politically significant. It complicated his situation with Octavia and his Roman family, but it showed his commitment to Cleopatra and their partnership.

Cleopatra became pregnant again. Their third child, Ptolemy Philadelphus, would be born later that year.

The Parthian Disaster

The Parthian campaign of 36 BCE was a catastrophe from start to finish.

Antony assembled a massive army. Ancient sources suggest 16 Roman legions plus auxiliary troops from client kingdoms, possibly totaling over 100,000 men. It was one of the largest armies Rome had ever fielded in the East. The logistics alone were staggering. Antony had to supply tens of thousands of soldiers with food, water, and equipment through hostile territory.

The campaign started poorly. Antony divided his forces, sending his baggage train, which included all the siege equipment, by a different route to speed his advance. This turned out to be a fatal mistake. The Parthian cavalry attacked and destroyed the baggage train, capturing or killing the guards and destroying the siege engines. Without siege equipment, Antony couldn't take fortified cities.

He pressed on anyway, besieging Phraaspa, the capital of Media Atropatene (a Parthian ally). The siege dragged on through the autumn. The Parthian cavalry constantly harassed his supply lines. His Armenian allies, led by King Artavasdes, eventually withdrew their support. Winter was approaching, and his soldiers were running out of food.

Finally, Antony had to admit defeat. He ordered a retreat. It turned into a nightmare. The Parthians pursued his army, constantly attacking. The terrain was harsh, and supplies ran low. Soldiers died from combat, disease, exposure, and starvation. Ancient sources claim he lost over twenty thousand men—possibly as much as a quarter of his army—during the retreat.

He limped back to Syria in the winter of 36/35 BCE, having accomplished nothing. He had won no territory. He took back no standards. He only suffered massive losses and a severely damaged reputation.

Throughout the ordeal and its aftermath, Cleopatra provided crucial support. She sent supplies, money, and clothing for his troops. When he reached the Syrian coast, she was waiting for him with resources to help rebuild his shattered army. Her support might have been what saved his campaign from being even worse, and it certainly increased his dependence on her.

The Propaganda War

While Antony struggled in Parthia, Octavian had been busy in Rome consolidating his power and building a narrative about his rival. The propaganda campaign against Antony and Cleopatra only intensified after the Parthian disaster.

Octavian portrayed Antony as a man who had abandoned Roman values for Eastern decadence. He had married a foreign queen (never mind that Cleopatra was Greek, not Egyptian). He had given Roman territories to a foreign power. He had also abandoned his virtuous Roman wife for a foreign seductress. Antony was even rumored to be planning to move the capital of Rome to Alexandria and rule as a monarch in the East.

Some of this was exaggeration, and some was outright fabrication. However, some had just enough truth to be effective. Antony really had given territories to Cleopatra's children. He really did spend most of his time in the East. He really had set aside Octavia for Cleopatra. After the Parthian disaster, he looked weak and un-Roman.

Octavia, to her credit, tried to help. In 35 BCE, she traveled east with supplies, money, and fresh troops for Antony in a public display of wifely devotion that would reflect well on him in Rome. But Antony didn't let her reach him. He sent messengers telling her to turn back. Some sources suggest he did this at Cleopatra's urging, not wanting his Egyptian queen and his Roman wife in the same city. Octavia returned to Rome rebuffed, but she refused to leave Antony's house. She maintained the appearance of a loyal wife even as her brother used her rejection as propaganda.

The Donations of Alexandria

In 34 BCE, Antony staged one of the most controversial acts of his career. He'd managed a minor victory in Armenia against the king who'd betrayed him. He captured King Artavasdes and decided to celebrate with a triumph. But instead of holding it in Rome, as tradition dictated, he held it in Alexandria.

The ceremony was a spectacle. Antony rode through Alexandria in a chariot, with the Armenian king in golden chains walking behind him. It was a deliberately Roman ceremony performed in an Egyptian city. Cleopatra watched from a golden throne, presented in the guise of the goddess Isis. The message was clear: Antony wanted to display his power in the East, even if this did not necessarily mean he saw Alexandria as his capital.

Then came the Donations of Alexandria. In a grand public ceremony, Antony crowned Cleopatra "Queen of Kings" and Caesarion "King of Kings. " He also publicly emphasized Caesarion's parentage, which implicitly challenged Octavian's claim as Caesar's legitimate heir. He distributed territories to Cleopatra's children as well. Alexander Helios received Armenia, Media, and Parthia (the last being aspirational rather than conquered territory). Cleopatra Selene received Cyrenaica and Crete, and Ptolemy Philadelphus received Syria and Cilicia.

These were Roman client territories or spheres of Roman influence. Antony had no legal authority to give them away, especially to the children of a foreign queen. It was an attempt to build a Hellenistic-style dynastic order in the East, with Cleopatra and her children at its center.

The reaction in Rome was explosive. Octavian had exactly the ammunition he needed. To Roman eyes, this was not just an alliance with a foreign monarch; it was a dangerous overreach. Antony appeared to be elevating a foreign dynasty and undermining Roman authority. The Senate didn't declare war yet, but the groundwork was being laid.

In 32 BCE, Antony formally divorced Octavia. He sent her notice to leave his house with their children. It was an insult to Octavia, an insult to Octavian, and a political gift to his rival. Octavian responded by reading what he claimed was Antony's will (how he obtained it remains uncertain—he probably extracted it from the Vestal Virgins, though whether every detail was genuine is debated). The will allegedly stated that Antony wished to be buried in Alexandria with Cleopatra rather than in Rome with his ancestors.

That did it. The Senate declared war. They didn't technically declare war on Antony. War was declared on Cleopatra. That was because Octavian couldn't officially declare war on a fellow Roman, so he framed it as a war against a foreign queen who had seduced and corrupted a Roman general. It was a political fiction. Everyone understood this was a struggle between Octavian and Antony, but the fiction allowed Octavian to pose himself as the defender of Rome against an external threat rather than as a participant in yet another civil war.

The stage was set for the final confrontation.

The Battle of Actium

In 31 BCE, the forces of Octavian faced off against the combined forces of Antony and Cleopatra in what would be the decisive battle of the Roman civil wars.

Antony and Cleopatra had established their base at Actium, on the western coast of Greece near the entrance to the Ambracian Gulf. It was a defensible position with access to the sea. They had assembled a substantial fleet, perhaps five hundred ships, including Cleopatra's Egyptian squadron. They also fielded an army of maybe sixty thousand to seventy thousand men. On paper, they were formidable.

But there were problems from the start. Octavian's general, Marcus Agrippa, was one of the finest naval commanders in Roman history. He established a blockade that cut off Antony's supply lines and captured several key coastal positions. Soldiers started deserting. Disease spread through the crowded camps. Morale deteriorated. And Antony's officers didn't trust Cleopatra. They saw her as a foreign queen who had led Antony away from Rome and Roman values.

The officers urged Antony to send Cleopatra back to Egypt and fight a land battle, where Roman legions traditionally excelled. However, Antony refused. Cleopatra had provided much of the fleet and significant financing. Her presence was politically important; this was their joint cause and their joint future. Besides, she controlled the war chest, and Antony needed her resources.

On September 2nd, 31 BCE, the naval battle began. The details are murky, and ancient sources conflict with each other, but the broad strokes are clear. Agrippa's fleet was more maneuverable. His ships used a new weapon called the harpax, a grappling device fired from a catapult that could lock onto enemy ships and pull them close for boarding. Antony's larger warships, designed for ramming, were at a disadvantage.

At some point during the battle—sources disagree on exactly when—Cleopatra's squadron of about sixty ships broke through the enemy line and sailed away, heading south toward Egypt. Antony, seeing this, abandoned his flagship and transferred to a smaller, faster ship to follow her. His fleet, seeing their commander flee, lost heart. Many ships surrendered. Others tried to escape. It was a rout.

Ancient sources debate Cleopatra's motivations and whether Antony's actions were planned or impulsive. Some claim it was a prearranged escape plan. Cleopatra was supposed to break through with the war chest, and Antony would follow to preserve their resources for continued resistance. Others claim Cleopatra panicked and fled, and Antony impetuously abandoned his men to chase after her. Still others suggest it was a tactical retreat that simply failed.

What's clear is that it looked terrible. A Roman general had abandoned his troops in the middle of battle to follow a foreign queen. Whether or not it was planned, whether or not there were good reasons, the optics were disastrous. Antony's remaining forces—both the fleet and the army camped on shore—soon surrendered to Octavian.

The Endgame

Antony and Cleopatra returned to Alexandria to find their world collapsing. Most of Antony's eastern allies quickly made peace with Octavian. There would be no coalition to resist him. They spent the winter of 31/30 BCE in a strange mixture of denial and preparation.

Ancient sources describe lavish parties and the creation of a new society called the "Partners in Death"—a grim echo of their earlier "Society of the Inimitable Livers." However, they were also desperately trying to find a way out. Cleopatra sent envoys to Octavian with gifts, trying to negotiate. She offered to abdicate in favor of her children if Octavian would let them rule Egypt as Roman clients. She even reportedly offered him vast sums of money.

Octavian's responses were calculated to divide them. He sent cold, noncommittal replies to Antony while sending more encouraging but vague messages to Cleopatra, suggesting she might save herself if she abandoned Antony. It was psychological warfare. He was trying to make each of them doubt the other's loyalty.

Cleopatra also made practical preparations. She had ships dragged overland to the Red Sea, apparently planning an escape to Arabia or even India if Alexandria fell. However, the plan failed when local Arab tribes, possibly acting independently or at Octavian's behest, burned the ships. She fortified her mausoleum—a tomb she had been building for herself—and moved Egypt's treasury there.

She also began collecting poisons. Different poisons kill in different ways. Some cause convulsions, screaming, and agony. Others were slower and involved hours of suffering. Cleopatra wanted something quick, painless, and dignified. According to ancient sources, she tested various poisons on condemned prisoners, observing the effects with clinical detachment. Which poisons caused pain? Which worked fastest? Which left the body looking peaceful, as if merely asleep? She was essentially conducting lethal experiments, and the condemned prisoners were her unwilling test subjects.

In the summer of 30 BCE, Octavian's forces arrived. He approached from both the west (across North Africa) and the east (through Syria). Egypt's former territories, the ones Antony had given Cleopatra's children, quickly submitted to Octavian. There would be no resistance from them.

Antony managed to win one small cavalry skirmish outside Alexandria, which briefly raised his spirits. However, when the decisive moment came, his remaining forces defected to Octavian without a fight. His fleet rowed out to engage Octavian's ships and then immediately raised their oars in salute and joined Octavian's side. His cavalry did the same. His infantry melted away. In a single day, Antony's army ceased to exist.

Antony retreated to Alexandria. Ancient sources describe him as distraught, ranting that Cleopatra had betrayed him. Whether he actually threatened her or this was simply his despair talking, Cleopatra retreated to her fortified mausoleum with her two handmaidens, Iras and Charmion, and had the doors sealed.

According to ancient sources, someone told Antony that Cleopatra was dead at some point after his army collapsed. Whether this was a mistake, a lie, or part of Cleopatra's own plan is unclear. Believing he had nothing left to live for, Antony attempted to commit suicide in the traditional Roman fashion. He ordered his servant Eros to kill him. When Eros refused and killed himself instead, Antony fell on his own sword.

But he botched it. The wound was fatal but not immediately so. He lay bleeding, calling for someone to finish him. Then word came that Cleopatra was alive, barricaded in her mausoleum. Antony asked to be carried there.

The mausoleum's doors were sealed, as Cleopatra feared Octavian's soldiers would break in if she opened them. So, Antony was hoisted up through a window with ropes. Plutarch describes it as undignified. The dying general was hauled up the side of a building while Cleopatra and her two handmaidens pulled on the ropes. He died in her arms. He was about fifty-three years old.

Cleopatra's Final Days

Cleopatra surrendered to Octavian after Antony's death, but she had no intention of being paraded through Rome in chains as her sister Arsinoe had been. Ancient sources say Octavian sent one of his officers, Cornelius Dolabella, to negotiate with her, and Dolabella, perhaps charmed by her or perhaps pitying her, warned her that Octavian planned to send her to Rome within days.

She asked permission to visit Antony's tomb and pour libations. Octavian agreed. She went with her two faithful handmaidens, Iras and Charmion, dressed in mourning. She made offerings at Antony's tomb, knowing it would be her last visit to him.

Then she returned to her chambers and requested a final meal. Ancient sources say a basket of figs arrived, brought by a peasant. Hidden in the figs was an asp, a small, venomous snake. Cleopatra wrote a letter to Octavian, asking to be buried with Antony, and had it sent to him.

By the time Octavian's guards had burst into her chambers, it was over. They found Cleopatra dead on her golden couch, dressed in her royal regalia. Iras lay dead at her feet. Charmion was dying, still trying to adjust the crown on her mistress's head. When the guards asked what had happened, Charmion supposedly said, "It is well done, and fitting for a princess descended of so many royal kings," before she too died.

The snake supposedly bit Cleopatra on the arm or breast. Modern historians debate whether it was really a snake. Asp venom isn't always quickly fatal, and Cleopatra had supposedly tested various poisons to find the best method. It might have been poison from another source, with the asp story added later for dramatic effect. What matters is that Cleopatra chose her death. She chose to die as queen of Egypt rather than live as Octavian's captive.

She was thirty-nine years old. It was August 12th, 30 BCE.

Octavian, according to sources, was angry that she had denied him his triumph. However, he granted her wish. She was buried with Antony in her mausoleum. The location of their tomb remains unknown to this day.

The Aftermath

With Cleopatra's death, the Ptolemaic dynasty ended after nearly three centuries. Egypt, which had maintained nominal independence as a Roman client kingdom, became a Roman province. It was essentially Augustus's personal property. No senator would be allowed to visit without the emperor's permission.

Octavian executed Caesarion shortly after. The young man was about seventeen. The official reason was that he posed a threat as a potential rival (as Caesar's alleged son), but really, Octavian couldn't afford any possible challengers. Ancient sources preserve the blunt advice he received: "Too many Caesars is not good." Cleopatra's three children with Antony—Alexander Helios, Cleopatra Selene, and Ptolemy Philadelphus—were spared and sent to Rome to be raised by Octavia, Antony's widow. She raised them alongside her own children with surprising kindness and dignity.

Cleopatra Selene eventually married King Juba II of Mauretania and became a queen in her own right. The historical record falls silent when it comes to her two brothers. We don't know what became of them. Most historians assume they died young, possibly from illness. It is also possible they were eliminated quietly before they could pose any political threat.

The era of the Hellenistic kingdoms was over. Rome would rule the Mediterranean unchallenged for centuries. Octavian, who would soon take the name Augustus, became the first Roman emperor. The Roman Republic was dead. The Roman Empire had begun.

Chapter 6 – Legacy

Queen of the Nile: Cleopatra's Reign

Cleopatra was much more than her relationships. Though her passionate affairs with Julius Caesar and Mark Antony have made her famous, her reign shows that she was also a shrewd politician and diplomat who managed to stabilize the troubled state of Egypt at the start of her rule. While it is debated how much long-term wealth she generated, her economic reforms and cultural patronage strengthened her kingdom's position, and it was partly due to Egypt's resources and strategic value that Octavian found Egypt so desirable as he campaigned through the Mediterranean.

Far from being merely a seductress, Cleopatra was an accomplished monarch who worked tirelessly to maintain Egypt's independence and prosperity in the face of Roman expansionism. However, this view was clouded by the successful propaganda campaign waged against her.

Egypt at the Start

Cleopatra had the benefit of co-ruling with her father, Ptolemy XII, at the beginning of her reign. Before she ascended to the throne as the sole ruler, she was already involved in administrative and political work. She had a strong understanding of the financial state Egypt was in. Cleopatra had witnessed her father's exile and his dependence on Roman support to reclaim his throne, and she would have known of the debt that had to be paid to the mercenary soldiers he used.

Cleopatra would also have been aware that her father was more of a hedonistic king than a practical one. She would have noticed that he didn't take an active hand in the administrative duties of the kingdom. Historians have found evidence that Cleopatra was a much more hands-on ruler, thanks to her known interventions in official decrees. This hands-on attitude might have come from her education or her observations while in exile with her father. While we cannot be completely sure of her motivations, it is clear that Cleopatra was deeply affected by the state of the kingdom, as she worked to secure a powerful position for Egypt in relation to the expanding Roman Republic.

In 51 BCE, Egypt was in a precarious financial position due to the substantial debts incurred by Ptolemy XII. In his struggle to retain the throne, he gave gifts and bribes to various Roman officials to buy their allegiance and keep them from annexing Egypt. These political interventions were costly, and Ptolemy XII was burdened with massive debts when he returned to the throne. To pay his creditors, he was forced to devalue the Egyptian currency and impose heavy taxes. The debts were so great that even when Cleopatra came to the throne and won the Alexandrian War, Caesar still demanded that she repay the remaining debts of her father.

Environmental Factors in Egypt

Ptolemy's debts were not the only factor that destabilized Egypt at the start of Cleopatra's reign. In 46 and 44 BCE, at least one major volcanic eruption likely changed the global climate enough to affect precipitation along the Nile. According to recent research, volcanic activity around that time might have weakened the monsoon winds, which were crucial for precipitation in eastern Africa that fed the Nile. This weakening of the monsoon systems has been linked to prolonged dry spells that kept the Nile from flooding. The annual flooding of the Nile was so crucial to Egyptian agriculture that it formed the basis for the Egyptian calendar. Without the Nile's flood, harvest yields were smaller, and famine swept throughout the kingdom. This, in turn, weakened the population of Egypt and disrupted trade patterns throughout the Mediterranean. It led to economic instability in Egypt, which relied on its agricultural exports, especially grain, to keep its economy going. It also caused significant social unrest as the government began to rely more heavily on taxation for revenue.

Administration and Government

By the time Cleopatra came to power, the administration of the Egyptian government was functional but strained. The upper levels of government had been staffed by Ptolemaic Greeks, but as Alexandria struggled through civil war after civil war, many key officials died or were assassinated, destabilizing certain parts of the government. The strict Ptolemaic administration could not operate at its normal efficiency since officials were replaced and struggled to maintain stability while the country was in crisis.

Agricultural output and trade were affected not only by environmental factors but also by political instability. The country could not function properly if it were constantly at war, and from 55 to 47 BCE, Egypt was embroiled in a series of civil wars and conflicts between claimants to the throne. Egypt possessed valuable resources, including grain and minerals, that were valuable to the Romans and gave Egypt a lot of economic leverage throughout the Mediterranean. But without a proper administration, secure government, and effective trade strategies in place, these resources could not be fully utilized. When Cleopatra finally secured the throne, she had the unenviable task of stabilizing the chaos in the administration and implementing strict reforms to return Egypt to the economic prosperity it was capable of achieving.

Cleopatra's Vision for a New Egypt

The first few years of Cleopatra's reign were spent fighting her younger brother for control of Alexandria. When this was over, she set about consolidating her rule. A major aspect of this was reforming the economy and administration of Egypt. As we have seen throughout this book, Cleopatra's goal was to maintain Egypt's independence while securing Rome's protection. It was a delicate balance that required Egypt to be valuable enough to Rome that they would not annex it but strong enough that it did not become completely dependent on Roman loans. She swiftly implemented a series of administrative reforms to revitalize Egypt's economy, along with a policy of cultural diplomacy to maintain her popularity in Egypt.

Economic Reforms

The first and most significant were the monetary reforms she put in place. During her father's reign, Cleopatra saw him debase (devalue) the Egyptian currency to pay his debts to Rome. Cleopatra changed the nature of bronze coins in circulation. She modified them so that the value of each coin was determined by Cleopatra's decree rather than the intrinsic value or weight of the metal in the coin. This was done to help align the value of Egyptian coinage more closely with the Roman denarius, the standard coin used throughout the Hellenistic world. This meant that no matter how much actual bronze was used to make one Ptolemaic bronze coin, it would still be valued at whatever Cleopatra decided it was worth. This was similar to the modern form of currency exchange.

Though this seemed to have stabilized the Egyptian economy to a certain extent, there was still some debasement of the Ptolemaic currency throughout her reign. By the end of her rule, her silver coins were at about 40 percent purity (40 percent of the coin was made up of the metal of its nominal value) compared to a Roman denarius at around 95 to 98 percent purity.

Cleopatra also strengthened the economy by maintaining price controls, upholding state monopolies on certain goods (textiles and papyrus, in particular), and enforcing laws to keep peasant farmers in their villages during the crucial planting and harvesting seasons. This stabilized Egypt's agricultural output and ensured that government officials would be able to accurately collect taxes based on the farmers' output. These measures were put into place after years of famine, during which Cleopatra took direct action by ordering the royal granaries to distribute food to the peasants. Reforms such as these helped prevent the population from revolting against Cleopatra and also strengthened her image as a benevolent and active ruler. This was in stark contrast to her father, who was seen as self-indulgent and ineffective.

Cultural Diplomacy

Throughout her life, Cleopatra was known to be an intelligent politician, skilled in the art of diplomacy. She reportedly spoke several languages and was the first Ptolemaic pharaoh known to speak Egyptian, which likely helped endear her to the population she ruled. A significant part of her legacy is her cultural awareness and her efforts to preserve Egyptian religion and cultural practices. As a pharaoh, she chose Isis as her divine counterpart, the goddess who represented motherhood and protection; this was as much a public relations choice as a personal one. Cleopatra wanted to be seen as the mother of her people because it would help solidify her power and earn her reverence within the kingdom.

She also aimed to elevate the status of Egyptian religion to enhance Egypt's prestige throughout the Mediterranean. During her reign, she supported the construction and restoration of temples honoring both Egyptian and Greek deities, appealing to both aspects of her diverse population. She is believed to have contributed to the Dendera Temple Complex in Upper Egypt, where reliefs depict her and her son, Caesarion, presenting offerings to the gods Hathor and Horus. She might also have supported construction at the Hathor-Isis Temple, where inscriptions appear in both ancient Greek and Demotic Egyptian, again including images of herself and Caesarion worshiping Egyptian gods. The most significant of these efforts was likely the Caesareum, a temple near the seafront of Alexandria, later dedicated to the worship of Julius Caesar. The entrance was later flanked by two giant granite obelisks, which came to be known as Cleopatra's Needles. She also ordered repairs to major structures in Alexandria that had been damaged during the Alexandrian War. Including her son in temple reliefs and honoring Caesar helped to reinforce and strengthen the legitimacy of her rule, her connection to Rome, and the cultural duality of the Ptolemaic state.

A hallmark of Ptolemaic rule had been artistic and cultural patronage, as evidenced by monuments built by previous kings, like the Lighthouse and the Great Library of Alexandria. By supporting public works and commissioning sculptures, such as depictions of Hathor and Caesarion, Cleopatra upheld the Ptolemaic tradition of encouraging the arts and blending cultures to create a unique identity. Under her reign, Alexandria remained a center of intellectual and artistic activity. While concrete evidence of her direct patronage is limited, she was known to engage with elite society and reportedly participated in private social circles such as the "Inimitable Livers." All of this enhanced her image as an enlightened ruler—that was, until her association with Mark Antony. The lavishness of their court gave her enemies the material they needed to turn public opinion against her.

Political Legacy

Cleopatra's most significant political accomplishment was maintaining Egypt's independence and wealth in the face of Roman encroachment. For twenty years, she skillfully navigated the complex political landscape of the Mediterranean during an era marked by back-to-back civil wars and dramatic power plays. She leveraged Egypt's resources and formed strategic alliances to secure her position as pharaoh.

Her diplomatic skills were most evident during her time with Caesar. Though their relationship was romanticized, at its core, it was a political alliance built on mutual benefit. Egypt provided Rome with crucial grain shipments, and Caesar's legions provided military support. Cleopatra even found strategic benefit in her passionate romance with Mark Antony. Though their union ended tragically, she briefly regained control of some eastern Mediterranean territories during their time together.

Cleopatra also gives us one of the earliest examples of public relations in history. She tailored her presentations to different audiences, knowing when to make dramatic entrances for maximum effect, as seen in her meetings with Caesar and Antony. She used gift-giving to demonstrate Egypt's wealth and influence to foreign powers, yet spoke Egyptian to communicate directly with her subjects. She developed a well-informed political strategy using trusted advisors and intelligence networks. While later historians would use these tactics as examples of her seductive behavior, from a modern perspective, it is clear that Cleopatra was a sophisticated political operator.

Her reign ultimately ended with Egypt's incorporation into the Roman Republic (although it would very soon become the Roman Empire), but her political shrewdness left a lasting legacy. She showed that a woman could rule a major power in the ancient world as effectively as her male peers. It has taken history a long time to unwind the propaganda set down by her enemies, but historians continue to shed new light on her reign. For instance, environmental upheaval once blamed on poor judgment is now understood to have resulted from volcanic activity that disrupted the Nile's flooding.

Legacy of a Legendary Queen

Cleopatra's legacy has been a subject of fascination, controversy, speculation, and reinterpretation since the moment she died. We know very little about her early life. Most of what we know is speculation based on what we understand of the Alexandrian elite and Ptolemaic royalty during the Hellenistic period. Her story has been twisted and untwisted by historians from ancient times to the modern day, always through the lens of various historical, political, and cultural forces. Whether you think of her as a seductress or a political genius, you cannot deny that the mystery surrounding Cleopatra has endured for over two thousand years, making her one of (if not the most) famous women in all of history.

Early Depictions of Cleopatra: Roman Propaganda

In the immediate aftermath of Cleopatra's death, her image was greatly skewed by Octavian's propaganda campaign. Octavian sought to discredit Cleopatra to justify his actions and ensure that the Antony-Cleopatra faction would no longer threaten Rome. He portrayed her as a dangerous foreign queen who had seduced both Caesar and Mark Antony and corrupted them, turning them against their Roman values. His narrative painted Cleopatra as a threat to Roman stability, emphasizing her extravagance, the hedonistic nature of her relationship with Mark Antony, her (alleged) manipulation of the men she had relationships with, and the exoticism of her Egyptian heritage. Roman writers of the time echoed themes consistent with Octavian's propaganda narrative. They portrayed her as a "femme fatale" who was a threat to Rome's dominance. In this way, Octavian managed to justify the annexation of Egypt without destroying his own character. Octavian appeared to offer clemency and pity toward his fellow countrymen, and in her death, Cleopatra became the villain of her own story.

Cleopatra's Story Begins to Evolve

The tide did not shift until the 1st century CE when Plutarch began to write his *Parallel Lives*. Meant to be a philosophical exploration and a way to provide moral and ethical instruction, Plutarch reexamined the lives of famous historical figures from the ancient world. He attempted to choose those figures whose lives paralleled one another and those from whom his audience could learn. Cleopatra was not a central figure in his book—she appeared in the volumes that explored Julius Caesar and Mark Antony's lives—but he provided a more nuanced portrayal of Cleopatra than those who had come before him.

Though Plutarch offers a somewhat more neutral portrayal of Cleopatra's intelligence and political skill, his account remains influenced by the gender and cultural stereotypes of his era. But still, he acknowledged her intelligence, wit, and diplomatic abilities. He was one of the first to recognize that Cleopatra was a polyglot. Plutarch presented her as a complex political figure rather than a one-dimensional villain, though he still emphasized her use of charm and personal appeal to influence powerful Roman men.

His portrayal of Cleopatra and Antony as a tragic love story went on to inspire many other works of literature and art. It is from Plutarch that we get many of the stories that are famous today, like the story about

Cleopatra sneaking into Caesar's quarters in a bed sack and the decadent image of Cleopatra, dressed as Aphrodite, sailing up the Cydnus to encounter Mark Antony. These stories, while iconic, should be understood as literary anecdotes rather than confirmed historical facts.

With Plutarch's account, historians and artists now had a more balanced perspective to draw from instead of the purely negative Roman propaganda. The balance between these interpretations shifted over time as societal morals, customs, and new discoveries shaped how writers looked at Cleopatra's story. For example, during the Middle Ages, a period of intense moral and religious piety, Cleopatra's life was often moralized and used as a cautionary tale about the dangers of lust and indulgence and the fleeting nature of worldly power. She was frequently depicted as a fallen queen, with her downfall attributed to her immorality, such as in Giovanni Boccaccio's *De Claris Mulieribus* (Latin: *Concerning Famous Women*). During the Renaissance, historians again began to reevaluate Cleopatra's legacy. They drew from Plutarch's portrayal and his description of Cleopatra as a witty and intelligent woman, and they began to portray her in a more sympathetic light that emphasized her passion, nobility, and political ability. This pendulum would swing back and forth during the Enlightenment and Romantic periods, reaching a peak in the Orientalism of the 19th century, which once again focused on Cleopatra as an exotic and sexual figure.

A woodcut illustration of Cleopatra and Antony from De Claris Mulieribus. The first scene is a banquet, while the second shows the two's deaths. [5]

Modern-Day Views of Cleopatra

To this day, Cleopatra continues to be a popular figure from antiquity, but modern scholars have changed their focus when examining her life. In recent decades, they have made efforts to reassess her historical legacy, challenging the long-held assumptions, stereotypes, and biases that have colored the popular perception of Cleopatra. In modern scholarship, Cleopatra's political acumen and her administrative and economic reforms have gained more prominence. The focus is now on Cleopatra as a capable ruler who navigated complex political relationships as she tried to defy Roman expansion. Feminist scholars have also reexamined Cleopatra's story. They were the ones to argue that the negative portrayal that has followed Cleopatra throughout history stems from sexist attitudes toward female leaders, pointing out that her ambition was often recast as ruthlessness. Meanwhile, these traits were admired in her male contemporaries, like Julius Caesar.

Racial Interpretations of Cleopatra

Debates about Cleopatra's ethnicity have gained prominence in recent years, with scholars arguing for a reexamination of how she is painted and portrayed and advocating for a more nuanced understanding of her Macedonian Greek heritage and how that interacted with Egyptian culture. Most recently, a documentary that depicts Cleopatra as Black has stirred up the controversy again, with some emphasizing that the modern understanding of "race" is a concept dating from the 18th century and that Cleopatra's life existed beyond that concept. In fact, Cleopatra was of Macedonian Greek heritage, and in the interest of consolidating power, the Ptolemies likely maintained that Greek heritage during their three hundred years of rule. However, there were gaps in the Ptolemaic dynasty tree that could have been filled by indigenous Egyptians, Romans, or other people from the Mediterranean and Middle East. The important thing to note is that the differences we see in these ethnicities today did not exist within the same context during Cleopatra's lifetime.

Historian Rebecca Futo Kennedy, writing in *Time Magazine*, makes an important point. We keep having the same argument about Cleopatra's race over and over instead of trying to understand how people in the ancient world actually thought about identity. Ancient artists depicted Cleopatra differently depending on whom they were creating the image for. They made her more Greek-looking for Greek audiences and more Egyptian-looking for Egyptian ones. This wasn't deceptive or contradictory. It reflected the reality that identity in the ancient Mediterranean was more fluid and context-dependent than our modern categories allow. By insisting on a single, definitive answer to "what race was Cleopatra," we are imposing 21st-century ideas onto a world that did not think in those terms.

Regardless of the color of her skin, Cleopatra showed that she deeply identified with her Egyptian heritage. She is the only member of the Ptolemaic dynasty known to have spoken the Egyptian language, and in much of her iconography, she associated herself with Egyptian gods and goddesses. In surviving artifacts like coins and busts, she is depicted as having curly hair and an aquiline nose, though the specific characteristics of her features are lost to history. The territory she once protected and fought for is now considered part of the Arab world, a change that happened gradually, beginning with the Arab Muslim conquest of Egypt in 641 CE, almost seven hundred years after she died. The primary language in the region is now Egyptian Arabic, which replaced Coptic (the latest stage of the ancient Egyptian language) by the 12th century. Even the idea of an "Arab world" is a modern concept, one that emerged in the mid-20th century.

In surviving busts and paintings from the 1st century CE, depictions of Cleopatra emphasize her Greek heritage. In one mural, she is painted as having pale, olive-toned skin and darker hair. This could be considered as accurate an account as we have of Cleopatra's skin color, but it is important to note that at this time, her Egyptian "otherness" would have been set aside in favor of a more "Greek" appearance.

The fact is, there is no definite answer to what was Cleopatra's "race" or skin color because her life has been clouded by bias from the beginning of its recorded

A mural of Cleopatra from the
1st century CE. '

history. In Rome, Cleopatra depicted herself as more Greek, while in Egypt, she was more Egyptian. The way we view her within the context of history swings back and forth between an exotic seductress and a shrewd politician, and there is no doubt the visual representations of Cleopatra were also colored by these shifting perceptions of her.

Cleopatra in the Art World: The Eternal Muse

If we were to list all of the paintings, sculptures, frescoes, and murals that have depicted Cleopatra and her life, this book would never end. She has been painted by artists throughout history and sculpted by those in her time and beyond, each honing in on a different aspect of her life. During her lifetime, Caesar is reported to have dedicated a bronze statue, possibly covered in gold, to Cleopatra and had it installed in the Temple of Venus Genetrix in Rome. Later, scenes from her life would be painted over and over again by artists from the Renaissance right up to the famous surrealist artist Salvador Dalí.

The Berlin Cleopatra

The earliest known depiction of Cleopatra and the one considered by some scholars to be the most accurate is the Berlin Cleopatra. The marble bust is dated to the mid-1st century BCE and is currently housed at the Altes Museum in Berlin, hence its name. The bust was likely sculpted around the time Cleopatra was in Rome, though its exact origin is uncertain, and its identification as Cleopatra is based on stylistic features and comparisons with coinage.

Its style and expression are, in their own ways, a nod to the two sides of her heritage. Her hair is

Berlin Cleopatra. [7]

styled in a signature "melon" hairstyle, with one knot at the neck and delicate curls protruding from the forehead, but she is also wearing the royal diadem of the Ptolemaic kings. Her face is sculpted in a serious manner, with a closed mouth and neutral expression, which is similar to other Greco-Roman busts sculpted around that time. Based on remnants left on the marble, scholars believe it may once have been covered in gold and was sculpted in two separate parts that were brought together.

Authentic, unromanticized depictions of Cleopatra are rare, making this bust extremely important for historians and scholars as a potential reference point for evaluating the accuracy of other paintings, sculptures, and frescoes featuring Cleopatra. It also provides them with insights into how the queen might have been perceived (retaining her Ptolemaic Egyptian characteristics while nodding to her Greek ancestry). The Berlin Cleopatra was unearthed at an ancient Roman villa along the Via Appia near Rome, and it was identified as a portrait of the queen in 1930. It has been on display at the Altes Museum in Berlin since 2010, where it sits beside the so-called Green Caesar.

Dante's *Inferno*

For many centuries after Cleopatra's death, she largely disappeared from visual art in Europe. While ancient Romans had depicted her in coins and possibly in frescoes or sculptures, the centuries after Rome's fall saw Cleopatra fade from artistic view. Christianity brought different priorities to art, like saints, biblical scenes, and religious stories. A pagan ruler associated with passion and luxury did not easily fit.

When Cleopatra did appear in medieval culture, it was more often in literature, and she wasn't portrayed kindly. One of the most famous and influential medieval depictions appears in Dante Alighieri's *Divine Comedy*, specifically the Inferno section, completed around 1314. Dante's epic poem takes readers on a journey through Hell, Purgatory, and Paradise. Each section of Hell is reserved for different categories of sinners, with punishments designed to fit the crime.

Cleopatra appears in Circle Two of Hell—the Circle of Lust. This circle is for people who let their desires overpower their reason, who are controlled by passion rather than being in control of it. She is in distinguished company: Dido, the queen of Carthage, who killed herself over Aeneas; Helen of Troy, whose beauty started the Trojan War; and Semiramis, the legendary Assyrian queen. Their sexuality led to their damnation.

The punishment Dante came up with for the lustful is both poetic and brutal. The souls are caught in a violent, eternal windstorm. Just like they were swept away by passion in life and couldn't control their desires, they're now swept away by winds forever, unable to control where they go. They can't talk to each other, can't rest, can't find any peace—just tossed around by forces beyond their control.

Dante's choice to put Cleopatra here is telling. He doesn't place her in the circles for fraud, treachery, or violence—sins you might associate with a ruler who had her siblings killed and who aligned herself with powerful Roman leaders for political gain. Instead, he focuses on her sexuality and her relationships with Caesar and Antony. In Dante's view, Cleopatra's defining sin was lust. She was a woman who let passion rule her, who was swept away by desire, and who couldn't control herself.

This reflects how medieval Christian culture often viewed female sexuality as morally dangerous and in need of strict control. Cleopatra became a symbol of what happened when women gave in to their desires—not just sexual desire but also ambition, power, and worldly pleasures. The Roman Catholic Church emphasized chastity, especially for women, and saw sexual passion as a distraction from spiritual devotion. Cleopatra, with her famous love affairs and her life filled with luxury and spectacle, represented many of the temptations medieval morality warned against.

Boccaccio's *Concerning Famous Women*

A few decades after Dante, another hugely influential text appeared: Giovanni Boccaccio's *Concerning Famous Women*, written between 1361 and 1362. This was one of the first collections of biographies focused exclusively on women, covering 106 women from Eve to Queen Joanna I of Naples. On the surface, it sounds progressive: an entire book about famous women at a time when women were rarely written about as historical figures. However, Boccaccio's purposes weren't exactly feminist. He used these biographical sketches primarily for moral instruction, and many of the women he included served as negative examples, warnings about the dangers of vice.

Cleopatra gets a prominent spot in *Concerning Famous Women*. Boccaccio presents her as an example of moral corruption. He acknowledges her intelligence and political skill, but he frames these qualities as dangerous because they were combined with her sexuality and ambition. In Boccaccio's telling, Cleopatra used her beauty and charm to seduce noble Roman men, corrupting them and leading them away from their duty to Rome. She represented luxury, indulgence, Eastern decadence, and the dangers of women wielding power.

Boccaccio describes Cleopatra as a fallen queen, and he attributes her downfall largely to her own character flaws. In his version, it wasn't Roman politics or military defeat that destroyed her; it was her own immorality. The moral of the story, for Boccaccio's medieval readers, was crystal clear: this is what happens when women step outside their proper place, when they seek power and pleasure, and when they refuse to be modest and chaste.

What's particularly interesting is how Boccaccio handles Cleopatra's intelligence. He doesn't deny it—the historical record was too clear. But he reframes it as dangerous. In his view, a clever woman is more dangerous than a foolish one because she can do more damage. Cleopatra's wit and political skill became weapons she used for immoral purposes. Where a male ruler might be praised for his intelligence and strategic thinking, Cleopatra's qualities are presented as evidence of her corrupting influence.

Concerning Famous Women was enormously popular. It was translated into multiple languages and widely read by educated Europeans for centuries. Boccaccio's portrayal of Cleopatra shaped how she would be understood for generations. Even writers who later took more sympathetic views of her had to respond to Boccaccio's influential negative portrait. His framing of her as a dangerous, lustful, ambitious woman who brought down great men became one of the most enduring interpretations.

Chaucer's *The Legend of Good Women*

Not every medieval writer took such a dim view of Cleopatra. Geoffrey Chaucer, writing his *Legend of Good Women* around 1386, offered a surprisingly sympathetic portrait that stood in stark contrast to Dante and Boccaccio. The poem was a collection of stories about women from classical literature and history, framed as a penance the narrator had to perform after writing negatively about women in his earlier works. The result is a fascinating document that presents famous women in a much more positive light than was typical for the period.

In Chaucer's version, Cleopatra's relationship with Antony isn't a tale of lust and corruption. It's a story of tragic romantic devotion. While Chaucer does not explicitly invoke the conventions of courtly love, his portrayal of Cleopatra emphasizes loyalty and sacrifice over seduction and manipulation. Cleopatra becomes a devoted lover, and Antony is a noble figure bound to her by love.

Chaucer essentially shifts Antony from one of Rome's most powerful men to the role of a tragic lover bound to Cleopatra, and he elevates her from a lustful figure to a martyr of love—someone who died for devotion and whose commitment was so absolute that she chose death rather than life without him. In Chaucer's telling, Cleopatra builds the tomb where she and Antony would be buried, fills it with serpents, and throws herself in after Antony's death, choosing to die among the snakes rather than live without him.

Modern scholars debate whether Chaucer's poem is sincere or satirical. Some read it as a genuine attempt to rehabilitate famous women who had been treated harshly by male writers. Others see it as a playful critique of literary conventions, using heightened language to parody the genre. The ambiguity is part of what makes it so interesting. But whether Chaucer meant it seriously or ironically, he created a version of Cleopatra that was very different from what his contemporaries were writing.

The Abreujamen Manuscript

Literature dominated medieval depictions of Cleopatra; visual representations were very rare. One remarkable exception appears in a 14th-century manuscript created at the papal court in Avignon, known as the *Abreujamen de las estorias.* This illuminated manuscript contains an image of Cleopatra that is unique and reveals medieval attitudes toward race, religion, and the enemies of Christianity.

In the *Abreujamen* illumination, Cleopatra is dressed as a European noblewoman, wearing the fashions of 14th-century aristocracy. However, the artist deliberately emphasized certain physical features, like her dark brown skin, conspicuously white teeth, and a rounded nose. This likely wasn't based on historical knowledge of what Cleopatra actually looked like.

The illuminator used these same racialized characteristics throughout the manuscript to depict other figures the medieval Christian world considered enemies. The entire Ptolemaic lineage is shown this way. So are ancient Persian kings and 12th-century Muslim leaders like Saladin. The artist appears to have linked Christianity's perceived enemies across more than a thousand years of history through shared physical characteristics that marked them as "Other," as outside the Christian community.

In medieval manuscripts, dark skin was used to mark enemies of Christianity. Cleopatra's inclusion here is particularly telling because she lived centuries before Christianity even existed and had no connection to the Crusades. But as queen of Egypt—the land of the pharaohs who enslaved the Israelites, where the Holy Family fled from Herod, and by the medieval period, a Muslim land—she could be lumped in with Christianity's enemies. In the medieval mind, these different "Egypts" all blurred together.

The *Abreujamen* manuscript is one of the very few known images in which Cleopatra is shown as anything other than a White woman. But we must remember this depiction was not an attempt at historical realism or a recognition of African ancestry. It was about using physical appearance as a visual for religious and political hostility. The artist wasn't trying to depict what Cleopatra might have looked like; he was trying to mark her as an enemy of Christianity.

The Boucicaut Master

The early 15th century marked the beginning of a transition. The Renaissance was starting to emerge in Italy and spread across Europe, bringing renewed interest in classical antiquity. Artists and scholars began studying ancient texts more carefully, and figures from Greek and Roman history became popular subjects. Around 1409, an artist known as the Boucicaut Master created an illumination of the tomb of Cleopatra VII and Mark Antony for a version of a work by Giovanni Boccaccio. It was one of the earliest visual representations of Cleopatra in many centuries.

The Boucicaut Master was an illuminator working in the early 1400s. He was probably French or Flemish. His name comes from a prayer book (a "book of hours") commissioned by Jean II Le Meingre, Marshal Boucicaut. Before the printing press, books were copied by hand, and wealthy patrons commissioned richly decorated manuscripts. Skilled illuminators like the Boucicaut Master were among the leading artists of their day.

The Boucicaut Master's illumination shows Cleopatra and Antony lying together in a Gothic-style tomb, with a snake near Cleopatra's chest and a sword through Antony's chest. Unlike earlier medieval works that used Cleopatra mainly as a moral lesson, this image treats her and Antony as historical figures in an actual story that involves love, tragedy, and death.

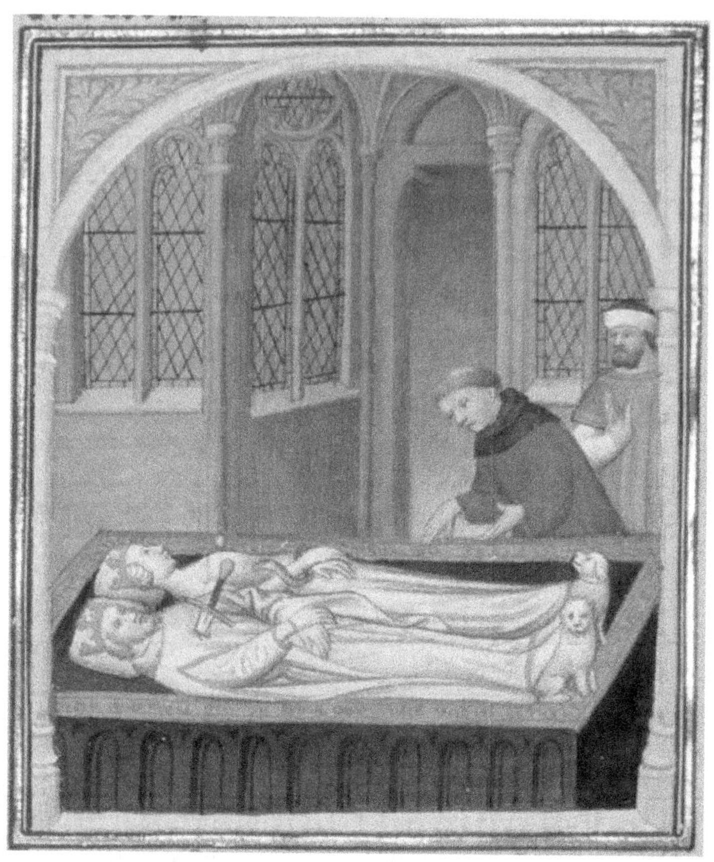

The Tomb of Cleopatra and Mark Antony. [8]

This shift was important. Medieval moralists like Dante and Boccaccio had been interested in Cleopatra primarily as an example or a warning. The specific details of her life mattered less than the moral lessons her story could teach. But the Boucicaut Master's illumination suggests a different approach, one more interested in the narrative and dramatic aspects of her life. This reflects the early Renaissance fascination with classical history, not just as a source of moral instruction but as something worth depicting for its own sake.

Because manuscripts were expensive, this kind of imagery would have been seen only by wealthy people who could commission such works. The fact that these patrons wanted images of Cleopatra suggests her story was becoming fashionable again among the aristocracy and educated classes. The medieval moralized version hadn't disappeared, but it was being joined by a growing interest in the drama and romance of classical antiquity.

Giampietrino's *Death of Cleopatra*

By the early 1500s, the Renaissance fascination with classical subjects was in full swing, and Cleopatra had become an acceptable—even desirable—subject for artists. Around 1515, the Italian painter Giampietrino created his *Death of Cleopatra,* a work that shows both the opportunities and the problems of how Renaissance artists approached her story.

Giampietrino was a follower of Leonardo da Vinci and worked in Milan. His painting shows Cleopatra at the moment of her death, but the way he depicts this moment is revealing. In the painting, Cleopatra is completely nude, reclining with her body on display. A snake—unmistakably phallic—bites her exposed breast. The viewer's eye is drawn not to her face or expression but to her body and the snake at her breast.

Death of Cleopatra by Giampietrino. [9]

This isn't a painting about Cleopatra's political defeat or her choice to die rather than be captured. It isn't about her dignity or defiance. It's an erotic image that connects female nudity, sexuality, and death together. The scene that should be about agency—Cleopatra choosing her own death rather than being paraded through Rome—becomes a voyeuristic spectacle. The woman who spent twenty-one years ruling Egypt, spoke multiple languages, and negotiated with Rome's most powerful men is reduced to a naked body for viewers to look at.

This approach established a pattern that would dominate Cleopatra's visual representation for centuries. The Renaissance brought her back into visual art after centuries of medieval moral warnings, but the paintings often cared more about displaying the female body than exploring who Cleopatra actually was or what her death meant. Art historians have noted that by the 17th century, patrons had the flexibility to commission works that pushed toward their own desires. If you wanted erotic art, asking for a painting of Cleopatra's death was perfectly respectable.

Artists also depicted Cleopatra according to European beauty standards. She has remarkably pale skin, often blonde or light brown hair, and delicate features that bear no resemblance to her actual Macedonian Greek heritage. Her death scene was consistently sexualized, and her story was told through a male gaze far more interested in spectacle and eroticism than in understanding the woman herself. Cleopatra would often be depicted reclining, often nude or semi-nude, with the snake as both a murder weapon and a phallic symbol. Her expression was either ecstatic or peaceful; it never showed pain or the actual horror of death by poison. These images told viewers that even in death, Cleopatra's primary function was to be beautiful and sexually available to the viewer's gaze. The Renaissance might have brought her back into art, but it reduced her to a single sexualized moment.

Jean Mignon's Cleopatra

In the mid-1500s, French artist Jean Mignon created an etching of Cleopatra's death that took a different approach from painters like Giampietrino. Where Giampietrino focused narrowly on Cleopatra's body, Mignon opted for an ornate, richly detailed scene. His etching is decorated with many elements, including a bedchamber, ornamental garlands, cherubs or putti, and a decorative frame that shows the story as part of a broader, symbol-laden composition.

Mignon belonged to the School of Fontainebleau, a group of artists at the French royal court known for elaborate and decorative works. These artists often treated classical and mythological themes with a sense of pageantry and lavish detail, which was in contrast to some Italian Renaissance works that emphasized more focused, dramatic moments.

Cleopatra Bitten by an Asp by Jean Mignon. [10]

In Mignon's etching, Cleopatra's death is shown as a dramatic, staged event, not just a private or erotic moment. The bed, the ornamental setting, the surrounding decorative elements, and the overall theatrical framing treat her death as a story steeped in luxury, symbolism, and spectacle. This treatment reinforces the idea of Cleopatra as excessive and indulgent, with her final moment surrounded by the trappings of luxury and material excess. The etching visualizes what older tales described in words. Unlike medieval texts that warned in abstract moral terms, Mignon showed that excess visually.

Mignon's work stands somewhere between medieval moralizing traditions and the Renaissance's revived fascination with classical stories. The etching does not seek to explore Cleopatra's politics or personality but to evoke a powerful story.

Cleopatra with the Asp - Guido Reni (c. 1628)

After disappearing from mainstream visual art for over a thousand years during the Middle Ages, Cleopatra returned in the early Renaissance, though often in problematic ways that sexualized her death. By the Baroque period, artists were creating more sophisticated interpretations that drew inspiration from Plutarch's *Parallel Lives.*

One of the most famous Baroque interpretations came from the Italian artist Guido Reni. The Renaissance had sparked renewed interest in figures and stories from classical antiquity, and Baroque artists took this further. The figure of Cleopatra was now regal and intellectual while still passionate and tragic—all elements that can be found in Reni's painting. The painting is infused with emotional intensity from the technique of chiaroscuro, which was used by many Baroque painters to convey drama and emotion and to guide the viewer's eye. The painting enhances Cleopatra's sense of loneliness as she meets her fate. Her body takes over the canvas, and the asp is a stark contrast to her skin. The painting manages to romanticize Cleopatra's tragic end without resorting to classic depictions of luxury and excess. It stands in stark contrast to Jean Mignon's etching from the 1500s.

Cleopatra with the Asp by Guido Reni. [11]

Cleopatra - John William Waterhouse (1888)

In the mid-1800s, the Western world experienced a renewed fascination with ancient cultures, but this time, they honed in on one period of classical antiquity. As more and more Europeans went on archaeological excavations in Egypt, the obsession with the ancient civilization grew. Fueled by discoveries like the Rosetta Stone, the continent was soon swept up in Egyptomania and began to incorporate Egyptian themes into Victorian-era art, literature, and decor.

John William Waterhouse, the pre-Raphaelite painter known for his romantic depictions of tragic heroines like Ophelia and the Lady of Shalott, added Cleopatra to his list of subjects, making her one of the few historical figures to receive his romantic treatment. The painting shows Waterhouse's signature style, blending elements of pre-Raphaelite and academic painting with a historical figure in a pose that emphasizes her intelligence, power, and sensuality.

Cleopatra by John William Waterhouse. [12]

Waterhouse paints Cleopatra sitting in her cushioned throne, her hand draped over a lion's head armrest. Her face is contemplative, yet her clothing is soft and shows the curves of her body beneath it. It tells the viewer that Waterhouse viewed Cleopatra as more than a tragic or sexual subject. The golden hues in Cleopatra's jewelry and surroundings are enough for the audience to get a sense of luxury and opulence, but her eyes remain the focal point, conveying a mix of intelligence and determination and engaging the viewer directly.

As a part of Waterhouse's catalog, Cleopatra stands out as a tragic figure who still has agency. Unlike Ophelia or the Lady of Shalott, she isn't staring up into the sky, pleading with someone. This is a very personal portrait, though it is not typical in Waterhouse's broader body of work. It is fitting for an age when women's roles were starting to be reexamined and when Britain was being ruled by its own complicated and tragic figure, Queen Victoria.

For a long time, scholars didn't know what happened to this painting. It was somewhat unusual in Waterhouse's body of work, as he didn't usually paint such intimate, close-up portraits, and they thought for a long time that it might have been destroyed. The painting resurfaced in the early 2000s in the collection of a man in Colorado, who claimed to have acquired it when he bought a business and its contents back in the 1960s. The painting was put up for auction and was estimated to sell at £500,000, but it did not reach its reserve price and remained unsold.

Cleopatra Before Caesar - Jean-Léon Gérôme (1866)

About two decades prior to Waterhouse's intensely emotional painting, Jean-Léon Gérôme produced a scene that shows Cleopatra in almost the opposite light. Gérôme's painting is practically a scene out of a film. In this work, Cleopatra's vulnerability comes from her exposure, with Gérôme using her light-colored body and clothing in contrast with the rich reds surrounding her to convey to the audience the potentially dangerous situation Cleopatra found herself in. Gérôme's painting brings to life a part of Cleopatra's myth that had rarely been shown in art—the moment she smuggled herself into Caesar's private chambers. This painting helped popularize that myth and contributed to making it feel like a historical fact. George Bernard Shaw drew on the "carpet" story, which appears in 18th-century translations of Plutarch, as inspiration for his play *Caesar and Cleopatra,* and the carpet myth carried over into film once Cleopatra's story crossed onto the silver screen.

Cleopatra Before Caesar by Jean-Léon Gérôme. [18]

While Gérôme's and Waterhouse's paintings come from the same period in history and are both influenced by the Egyptomania of the time, Waterhouse's depiction of Cleopatra is more intimate and subtly emphasizes Cleopatra's intellect and political acumen. Gérôme's, on the other hand, is more focused on Cleopatra's sensuality and the dramatic elements of her story. He shows us the Cleopatra who was committed to spectacle and indulgence, from the elaborately detailed Persian carpet to the fact that her breasts are partially visible in her loose dress.

Each of these paintings shows us how the different elements of Cleopatra's life story have been emphasized at different points in time. Whether it is a cautionary tale, as with Jean Mignon's etching, or a renewed focus on Cleopatra as a powerful female figure, Cleopatra has been a muse throughout history and a vessel for artists to explore modern ideas.

Cleopatra on Stage and Screen

It would take longer for Cleopatra to be reimagined for the stage. Painters could use her as an allegory for good and evil or for the dangers of indulgence versus chastity, but as dramatic as her story was, it would take a few hundred years before it was widely adapted for the stage. Once Shakespeare broke the seal on dramatizing the events of Cleopatra's life, audiences and dramatists alike could not get enough. The first was an almost cautionary tale of tragedy and the inevitability of fate. Later on, George Bernard Shaw would use Cleopatra as he did other historical figures: as a vessel for exploring his own politics and philosophy, though he would use Cleopatra's shrewd political ability to examine gender politics and the relationships between men and women. When Cleopatra finally appeared on the silver screen, artists and directors were finally able to truly convey the luxurious riches of her time.

Cleopatra was as much a pop culture figure as she was a historical one. This wasn't anything new. The British and French had glamorized her life in the 19th century as they excavated the riches of the ancient Egyptian world. In the 20th century, it was Hollywood's turn to do the same. From the beginning, Cleopatra was synonymous with excess and wealth, and in a way, her story finally came of age as the modern world turned to examine Cleopatra as a human rather than a goddess.

Antony and Cleopatra and *Caesar and Cleopatra*

The two major works about Cleopatra's life, ironically, focus on the two major relationships she had. Shakespeare's *Antony and Cleopatra* and George Bernard Shaw's *Caesar and Cleopatra* dramatize two significant periods in Cleopatra's life, but they differ considerably in their approach and thematic focus. For starters, the two playwrights didn't necessarily use or treat the source material in the same way. Shakespeare's main source would have been Plutarch's *Parallel Lives*. While Shaw might have used the same source, it would have been a different translation (likely the Langhorne translation, which was among the first to describe Cleopatra's arrival in a carpet rather than a bedding sack). The one Shakespeare used was probably Thomas North's translation, which was rendered from Greek into French before being translated into English. In both cases, parts of Cleopatra's story were lost or embellished for dramatic effect.

Shakespeare's play explores the themes of passion, power, and conflict, while Shaw's presents a more focused view of the political and intellectual mentorship between Caesar and Cleopatra. Shakespeare's play treats Cleopatra and Antony as one of history's great tragic romances, reinforcing the image of Cleopatra as a seductive queen. The play also follows the same basic narrative that Octavian promoted and that medieval writers used: Cleopatra's relationship with Antony is a cautionary tale about passion and downfall.

As far as tragedies go, Shakespeare's is more straightforward. We see two characters fall in love, fall to their hubris, and then fall on themselves. The image of Cleopatra as a seductress and the emphasis on the luxury of her life would have been more entertaining for audiences as well, and Shakespeare was known to be a playwright who wrote for the masses rather than for philosophical inquiry. A play about hubris was entertaining if you fell in love with the characters and empathized with their downfall. Shaw, on the other hand, was a more philosophical and political writer. It makes sense that he wrote a play about Cleopatra's more political relationship since, as a writer, Shaw often used the characters in his plays as a mouthpiece for his own ideas.

Shaw's play was less historically accurate, but it digs into power and politics in a way Shakespeare's doesn't. Shakespeare's play stuck closer to Plutarch's version of events, but he made them dramatic by covering a huge geographical area and a long timespan, using shorter scenes and poetic language to pull the audience into a story that was about more than just politics. Shaw did the opposite. He kept the setting focused on a shorter period and fewer characters so he could bend the facts to fit his themes about power and politics. He used more straightforward language that his audience could easily understand, with humor mixed in to make it digestible. Neither play is a biography. Both writers changed Cleopatra's life to fit their dramatic purposes, and both relied on Plutarch's account, which was told from the perspective of the men around her. We don't get Cleopatra's view of her relationships with Caesar and Antony because Plutarch only wrote about her as a side character in their stories.

The two plays made a huge impact on how Cleopatra has been portrayed ever since, though. They have been reinterpreted over and over throughout the 20th and 21st centuries. Shakespeare's work presents an older, more emotionally complicated Cleopatra in a sweeping historical drama, while Shaw's play shows her as a young woman learning politics. Together, they let us explore why Cleopatra's story has remained so fascinating and the different ways her life can be turned into drama. Without these plays, we might not have gotten the most famous depictions of Cleopatra on film, and she might not have become the pop culture icon she is today.

Cleopatra on Film

If there are two things that make films about Cleopatra stand out, they are the budget and the cultural impact. Once directors and actresses began to translate Cleopatra's story to the silver screen, her impact became much greater than ever before. True, she had been the subject of art for centuries, but this new interpretation came with an emotional element that had been missing. Until the 20th century, Cleopatra was seen through an artist's eyes, and her story was told as if it were a myth or an allegory. Through the cinematic portrayals of the 20th century, we gained a new understanding of Cleopatra through the actresses who played her, giving us a more nuanced look at her emotions and determination. With that came the grandeur of Hollywood and ancient Egypt, two places where you couldn't get enough of gold, silk, and a good story.

Cleopatra in the Silent Age

The first depiction of Cleopatra on screen was actually in 1899, when the film pioneer Georges Méliès made *Robbing Cleopatra's Tomb*, a short horror film in which a character named Cleopatra appears as a ghost or resurrected mummy. In 1912, American actress Helen Gardner produced and starred in a silent film titled *Cleopatra,* one of the earliest feature-length films in the United States. Gardner's Cleopatra was portrayed as a strong and calculating femme fatale, and the film was notable for its elaborate costumes and sets, many of which Gardner designed herself.

HELEN GARDNER AS "CLEOPATRA"

Helen Gardner in Cleopatra. [14]

In 1917, Theda Bara appeared in a silent film that was a combination of the adaptations by Shakespeare and the French playwrights Émile Moreau and Victorien Sardou. This film was partially lost, but some film stills remain depicting Bara as Cleopatra. She wears costumes clearly influenced by the Victorian Orientalist view of the queen. This is the first in a long line of Cleopatra adaptations that pushed the boundaries of budget and excess, with a budget of up to $500,000 (equivalent to about $12 million today). The production built copies of the Great Pyramid and the Great Sphinx of Giza, contracted a fleet of ships in the Balboa Peninsula, and had over fifteen thousand extras and two thousand horses. For the silent film era, this was one of the most expensive films ever made.

Theda Bara as Cleopatra. [15]

Because we don't have much of the film, it is difficult to make an analysis of how Theda Bara portrayed Cleopatra. However, in the 1930s, Hollywood brought Cleopatra back to the screen. One notable interpretation from that era was Claudette Colbert's portrayal in Cecil B. DeMille's *Cleopatra* (1934), a film not directly based on any single historical source but still shows the classic scenes of Cleopatra's life, namely her first encounter with Caesar. Colbert portrayed a seductive and cunning version of Cleopatra, an interpretation fitting for the glamour and excess of 1930s Hollywood. The film is memorable for its sensual sets and atmosphere, fitting right in with other DeMille movies.

Famous Actresses and a Famous Name

The next two women to play Cleopatra were already famous, strong, and complicated women themselves, and each gave a performance that was both influential and culturally impactful. Vivien Leigh and Elizabeth Taylor were two actresses who, although they were from different generations, were known to be beautiful, complex women who gave iconic performances. Leigh, with the iconic role of Scarlett O'Hara under her belt, partnered with Claude Rains, who played Caesar, in a film adapted from the George Bernard

Vivian Leigh as Cleopatra. [16]

Shaw play. Leigh's performance differs from other, more glamorous portrayals of Cleopatra, as she offers a more nuanced portrayal of the character. Leigh's Cleopatra isn't fully formed; she transforms before the audience's eyes from an ambitious but naive young woman to a formidable leader and a queen. Before this point, people usually focused on Cleopatra as a fully formed queen, one who seemed to roll out of the carpet as a political genius. In this portrayal, the audience watches as Caesar molds Cleopatra's instincts, leaving them wondering who is manipulating whom.

In Elizabeth Taylor's epic film, we see a very different Cleopatra. Taylor presents Cleopatra as a powerful, seductive, and politically astute queen. She does not offer the same vulnerability; instead, she shows the audience Cleopatra's charm, intelligence, and allure. The most impactful part of this performance, however, might have been the allure of what was going on behind the scenes. The film was among the most expensive films ever made up to that point, with a production cost that ultimately reached about thirty million dollars (with some reports estimating total expenditures, including reshoots and overruns, at around forty-four million dollars). The cost overruns nearly bankrupted the studio. Taylor and her co-star Richard Burton's intense on-screen chemistry spilled over onto set, and the pair became embroiled in a widely publicized affair that would remain one of the most-talked-about relationships in the history of Hollywood. After the film was released, the decadent sets, lavish costumes, and Taylor's Cleopatra became iconic, contributing significantly to the film's cultural legacy.

Elizabeth Taylor as Cleopatra. [17]

The women who played Cleopatra on screen embodied the fascinating complexities of her character in an age when feminism and evolving cultural attitudes began to influence how history's figures were reimagined for modern audiences.

Conclusion

We began this journey in the shadow of the great Ptolemaic pharaohs—Ptolemy I Soter, who built a kingdom from the ashes of Alexander the Great's empire, and Ptolemy II Philadelphus, who made Alexandria the intellectual crown jewel of the ancient world. We watched as that dynasty slowly crumbled through civil wars, weakened by debt and Roman encroachment, until it produced one final remarkable ruler: Cleopatra VII Thea Philopator.

She was born into a kingdom in crisis, exiled as a teenager, and forced to fight her own siblings for the throne. She allied with Julius Caesar and watched him die. She rebuilt her kingdom's prosperity through shrewd economic reforms while famine ravaged the land. She gambled everything on Mark Antony and lost. And when she knew the end had come, she chose to die on her own terms rather than be paraded through Rome in chains.

Cleopatra's life bridged the twilight of the Hellenistic era and the dawn of the Roman Empire. For twenty-one years, she kept Egypt independent through her intelligence, diplomacy, and sheer determination. She was the only Ptolemaic ruler who bothered to learn Egyptian and could speak to her subjects without a translator. She was an educated woman in a world that often didn't value female intellect. She practiced what we would now call public relations, tailoring her image to different audiences and making dramatic entrances when they would have maximum effect. She understood instinctively that politics is performance.

Her relationships with Julius Caesar and Mark Antony have overshadowed everything else about her for two thousand years. The truth is more complex than the narratives. These relationships were fundamentally political. They were strategic alliances between a queen fighting for her kingdom's survival and Roman strongmen who needed Egypt's wealth. But they were also genuine. Caesar and Antony weren't mindless puppets. They were two of the most brilliant, ambitious men of their age, and they chose Cleopatra as their partner for reasons that went beyond cold calculation. She matched them intellectually, understood their ambitions, and shared their vision of what the Mediterranean world could become.

Sometimes her calculations failed. Her commitment to Mark Antony in the 30s BCE, when Octavian was clearly winning Rome's final civil war, marked the beginning of her downfall. The Battle of Actium in 31 BCE sealed her fate. She had worked her entire adult life to secure Egypt's independence, to protect her children's inheritance, and to prove that a Hellenistic kingdom could survive in Rome's shadow. In the end, she realized she had bet on the wrong man and miscalculated Rome's internal politics. There was nothing left to do but orchestrate one final dramatic scene—dying on her golden couch in royal regalia, the asp hidden in a basket of figs, poison coursing through her veins as Roman soldiers battered at the mausoleum doors.

Beneath all the myth and propaganda, there was a real woman. She grew up in a palace where siblings were rivals, and murder was policy. She received the finest education available in the ancient world. She was exiled at twenty-one and had to build an army to reclaim her throne. She smuggled herself into Julius Caesar's presence (perhaps in a sack) because she understood that fortune favors the bold. She gave birth to four children. She made brilliant decisions and catastrophic miscalculations. She was fully human. Cleopatra was neither the monster her Roman enemies painted nor the perfect feminist icon modern admirers might wish her to be.

Modern historians have worked hard to separate fact from fiction. We now understand how Octavian's smear campaign shaped the ancient sources, how Plutarch's focus on great men relegated Cleopatra to a supporting role, and how each era's biases influenced its portrait of her. This book has tried to give a more nuanced picture—a queen who was genuinely brilliant but also ruthless, politically astute but also sometimes wrong, genuinely in love but also calculating, devoted to Egypt's independence but also willing to kill her siblings to secure power. She was a leader trying to save her kingdom in an age when kingdoms like hers were being overtaken by Rome.

The Ptolemaic dynasty ended with Cleopatra. After her death, Egypt became just another Roman province. The Great Library eventually burned down or fell into disrepair. The Mouseion declined. The Roman Empire would last another five centuries in the west, another thousand years in the east, but it would be a different kind of empire. It was more brutal, more efficient, and less interested in the cultural synthesis that had made Alexandria so remarkable.

Over two millennia, Cleopatra has been transformed from a historical figure into a myth, becoming a mirror in which each civilization sees its own values reflected back. Medieval Christians saw her as a cautionary tale about sin. Renaissance artists reimagined her as a tragic romantic figure. Victorians saw her as an example of exotic Eastern decadence. Modern feminists see her as a powerful woman destroyed by male propaganda. Each interpretation tells us as much about the interpreters as it does about Cleopatra herself.

This is her true legacy—not her dramatic life or tragic death but her ability to make us think. For over two thousand years, people have argued about her character, her choices, her loves, and her ambitions. Was she a victim of Roman imperialism or an ambitious player in Mediterranean power politics? Was she a brilliant ruler or someone whose charisma exceeded her judgment? Did she genuinely love Caesar and Antony, or were they useful allies? These questions have no simple answers, and that's precisely why Cleopatra endures when so many other historical figures have faded into footnotes.

Here was a woman who refused to be conquered, even when conquest was inevitable. She played the game as well as it could be played. She lost, but she made sure that her loss would be remembered as something magnificent. She understood that how we are remembered matters as much as how we lived. She was right.

Here's another book by Enthralling History that you might like

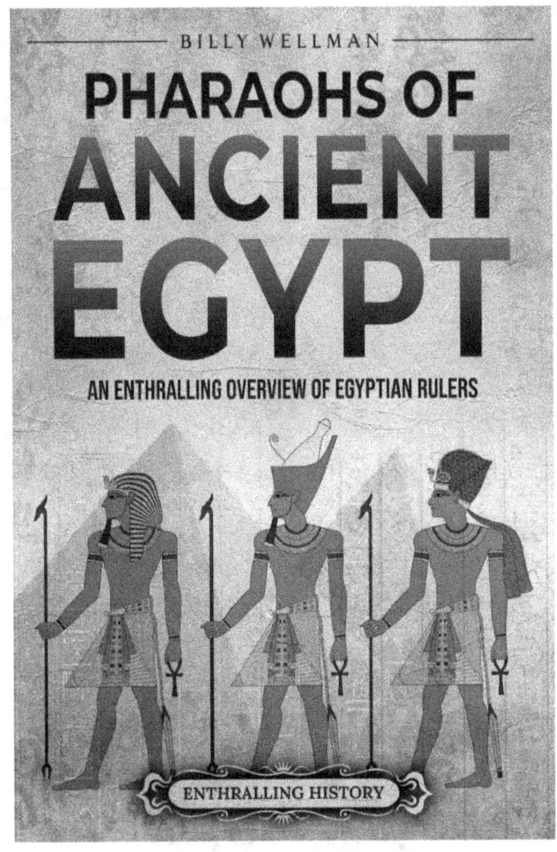

Free limited time bonus

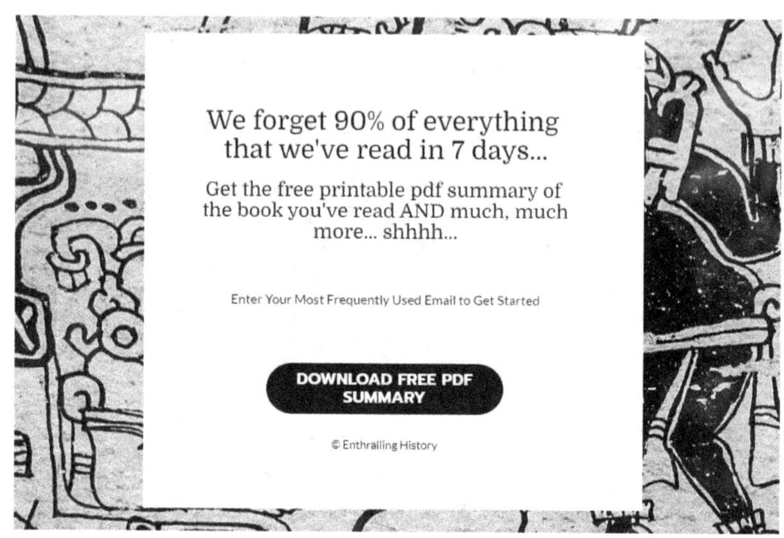

Stop for a moment. We have a free bonus set up for you. The problem is this: we forget 90% of everything that we read after 7 days. Crazy fact, right? Here's the solution: we've created a printable, 1-page pdf summary for this book that you're reading now. All you have to do to get your free pdf summary is to go to the following website: **https://livetolearn.lpages.co/enthrallinghistory/**

Or, Scan the QR code!

Once you do, it will be intuitive. Enjoy, and thank you!

Bibliography

"Antony against Parthia." Roman History 31 BC - AD 117, 12 Sept. 2017, https://ancientromanhistory31-14.com/an-end-of-the-republic/triumvirs/acts-of-the-triumvirs/antony-against-parthia/.

"Antony, Octavian, Cleopatra." Www.vroma.org, www.vroma.org/vromans/bmcmanus/antony.html.

BBC. BBC - History - Cleopatra. 2014, www.bbc.co.uk/history/historic_figures/cleopatra.shtml.

"Behind the Throne: Exploring the Life and Reign of Queen Cleopatra of Egypt." Www.memphistours.com, www.memphistours.com/Egypt/Egypt-Wikis/Egypt-History/wiki/queen-cleopatra-of-egypt.

Bianchi, Bob. "Cleopatra the Great: Last Power of the Ptolemaic Dynasty." ARCE, 2023, arce.org/resource/cleopatra-great-last-power-ptolemaic-dynasty/.

Bileta, Vedran. "The Battle of Actium: The Death of Ptolemaic Egypt." TheCollector, 2 Oct. 2021, www.thecollector.com/battle-of-actium/.

Blakemore, Erin. "Who Was Cleopatra?" National Geographic, 28 Apr. 2023, www.nationalgeographic.com/history/article/cleopatra-egypt-pharaoh-life-history.

Bowen, Shannon. "PR Prose: Cleopatra: The Queen of Public Relations? - College of Information and Communications | University of South Carolina." Sc.edu, 6 May 2016, https://sc.edu/study/colleges_schools/cic/journalism_and_mass_communications/news/2016/pr_prose_cleopatra_queen_of_pr.php.

Bowen, Shannon A. "Finding Strategic Communication & Diverse Leadership in the Ancient World: The Case of Queen Cleopatra VII, the Last Pharaoh of Egypt." Cogent Arts & Humanities, vol. 3, no. 1, 18 Mar. 2016,

www.tandfonline.com/doi/full/10.1080/23311983.2016.1154704,
https://doi.org/10.1080/23311983.2016.1154704.

Bressan, David. "How a Climate-Changing Volcano Helped the Roman Conquest of Egypt." Forbes, 2 Sept. 2019, www.forbes.com/sites/davidbressan/2017/10/18/demise-of-ancient-egypt-linked-to-a-climate-changing-volcano/. Accessed 6 Sept. 2024.

Britannica. "Cleopatra's Achievements." Encyclopedia Britannica, 23 Sept. 2020, www.britannica.com/summary/Cleopatras-Achievements.

British Museum. "Explore the Rosetta Stone." The British Museum, www.britishmuseum.org/collection/egypt/explore-rosetta-stone.

Brooke, Thomas. "The Siblings of Cleopatra, a Family like No Other...." Historical Novels and Epic Fantasy, 7 Oct. 2015, https://thomasmdbrooke.com/2015/10/07/the-siblings-of-cleopatra-a-family-like-no-other/

Christiansen, Keith. "Cleopatra, the Ultimate Femme Fatale." The Metropolitan Museum of Art, 18 Feb. 2017, www.metmuseum.org/articles/cleopatra-guido-cagnacci.

"Cleopatra." BBC, 2 Dec. 2010, www.bbc.co.uk/programmes/b00w7clj.

"Cleopatra and Mark Antony's Decadent Love Affair." History, 13 Feb. 2019, www.nationalgeographic.com/history/history-magazine/article/antony-and-cleopatra.

"Cleopatra the Beauty - Unknown." Google Arts & Culture, https://artsandculture.google.com/asset/cleopatra-the-beauty-unknown/bQEBFTu0tOisaw?hl=en.%20%E2%80%9CCleopatra%3A%20Rome%20and%20Egypt%2C%2069%E2%80%9330%20BC%20OCR%20Teachers%E2%80%99%20Guide.%E2%80%9D%20Warwick.ac.uk%2C%20warwick.ac.uk%2Ffac%2Farts%2Fclassics%2Fwarwickclassicsnetwork%2Fstoa%2Fanchist%2Fgcse%2Fcleopatra%2Fteachersguide%2F

"Cleopatra: What Is the Real Legacy of the Last Pharaoh?" HistoryExtra, www.historyextra.com/period/ancient-egypt/cleopatra-legacy-last-pharaoh-ptolemaic-dynasty/.

"Cleopatra's Impact on Rome: Politics, Culture, and Fashion." AncientScholar, 30 July 2024, ancientscholar.org/cleopatras-impact-on-rome-politics-culture-and-fashion/. Accessed 6 Sept. 2024.

"Cleopatra's Death." Uchicago.edu, 2019, https://penelope.uchicago.edu/~grout/encyclopaedia_romana/miscellanea/cleopatra/rixens.html.

Cohen, Alina. "How Millennia of Cleopatra Portrayals Reveal Evolving Perceptions of Sex, Women, and Race." Artsy, 6 May 2018, www.artsy.net/article/artsy-editorial-millennia-cleopatra-portrayals-reveal-evolving-perceptions-sex-women-race.

Cook, M. Climate Contributed to the Fall of Egyptian Dynasty | Real Archaeology. 29 Oct. 2017, pages.vassar.edu/realarchaeology/2017/10/29/climate-contributed-to-the-fall-of-egyptian-dynasty/.

Dowson, Thomas. "Green Caesar & Cleopatra in the Altes Museum, Berlin." Archaeology Travel, 27 Mar. 2023, https://archaeology-travel.com/artefacts/green-caesar-cleopatra/.

Fichter, Kero. "Constructing Racism in Western Art – Hans Makart and the Case of Cleopatra." DailyArt Magazine, 29 Apr. 2024, www.dailyartmagazine.com/the-case-of-cleopatra-constructing-racism-in-western-art/. Accessed 6 Sept. 2024.

Gouck, Michael. "Victorian Egyptomania: Why Was England so Obsessed with Egypt?" TheCollector, 22 Aug. 2022, www.thecollector.com/victorian-egyptomania/.

Haughton, Brian. "Cleopatra & Antony." World History Encyclopedia, 10 Jan. 2011, www.worldhistory.org/article/197/cleopatra--antony/.

---. "Cleopatra & Antony." World History Encyclopedia, 10 Jan. 2011, www.worldhistory.org/article/197/cleopatra--antony/.

health, William Wan National correspondent covering, et al. "Ancient Egypt's Rulers Mishandled Climate Disasters. Then the People Revolted." Washington Post, 17 Oct. 2017, www.washingtonpost.com/news/energy-environment/wp/2017/10/17/climate-change-sparked-revolts-in-ancient-egypt-study-says/.

Hill, Marsha. "Egypt in the Ptolemaic Period." Metmuseum.org, 2019, www.metmuseum.org/toah/hd/ptol/hd_ptol.htm.

Hillard, T. W. "The Nile Cruise of Cleopatra and Caesar." The Classical Quarterly, vol. 52, no. 2, Dec. 2002, pp. 549–554, https://doi.org/10.1093/cq/52.2.549. Accessed 22 May 2019.

History Extra. "Cleopatra, Julius Caesar and Mark Antony: How the Last Pharaoh's Love Affairs Shaped Ancient Egypt's Fate." HistoryExtra, 21 Aug. 2020, www.historyextra.com/period/ancient-egypt/cleopatra-love-affairs-julius-caesar-mark-antony/. Accessed 22 May 2019.

Holmes, Robert C. L. "Caesar under Siege: What Happened during the Alexandrine War 48-47BC?" TheCollector, 15 Nov. 2020, www.thecollector.com/julius-caesar-siege-of-alexandria-war/.

https://www.facebook.com/thoughtcodotcom. "Cleopatra's Family Tree Has Few Branches." ThoughtCo, 2019, www.thoughtco.com/queen-cleopatras-family-tree-4083409.

Huang, Shuoheng. Cleopatra's Autonomy as Ruler of Ptolemy Egypt and the Examination of the Roman Influence over Egypt. Shenzhen College of International Education.

"Julius Caesar, Cleopatra and the Alexandrian War | UNRV.com." Www.unrv.com, www.unrv.com/julius-caesar/cleopatra-alexandrian-war.php.

Kennedy, Maev, et al. "Victorian Masterpiece Turns up in Rocky Mountain Log Cabin." The Guardian, 31 May 2003, www.theguardian.com/uk/2003/may/31/arts.world.

Lary, Morris H. "Julius Caesar and Cleopatra: The Ancient World's Power Couple | History Cooperative." History Cooperative, 16 Aug. 2023, https://historycooperative.org/julius-caesar-and-cleopatra/

Little, Becky. "Cleopatra's Complicated Inner Circle: Siblings, Successors and Lovers." HISTORY, 13 July 2023, www.history.com/news/cleopatras-complicated-inner-circle-siblings-successors-and-lovers.

Mark, Joshua. "Cleopatra VII." World History Encyclopedia, 30 Oct. 2018, www.worldhistory.org/Cleopatra_VII/.

Mark, Joshua J. "Battle of Actium." World History Encyclopedia, 18 Nov. 2019, www.worldhistory.org/Battle_of_Actium/.

Marshall, Cynthia. "A Modern Perspective: Antony and Cleopatra | Folger Shakespeare Library." Www.folger.edu, www.folger.edu/explore/shakespeares-works/antony-and-cleopatra/antony-and-cleopatra-a-modern-perspective/.

McEvoy, Colin. "As a Ruler, Cleopatra Was as Charismatic as She Was Ruthless." Biography, 10 May 2023, www.biography.com/royalty/a43842745/was-cleopatra-a-good-ruler.

Milligan, Mark. "The Early Life of Cleopatra." HeritageDaily - Archaeology News, 24 Dec. 2021, www.heritagedaily.com/2021/12/the-early-life-of-cleopatra/142343.

Muhs, Brian. "The Ptolemaic Period (332–30 BCE)." The Ancient Egyptian Economy: 3000–30 BCE. Cambridge: Cambridge University Press, 2016. 211–252. Print.

"Mural of Cleopatra and Caesarion as Venus and Cupid." World History Encyclopedia, www.worldhistory.org/image/8287/mural-of-cleopatra-and-caesarion-as-venus-and-cupi/.

Nestruck, Kelly. "A Shaw Thing in Stratford-Upon-Ontario." The Guardian, The Guardian, 11 Sept. 2008, www.theguardian.com/culture/2008/sep/11/shakespeare.theatre.stratford. Accessed 6 Sept. 2024.

Owen Jarus. "Cleopatra: Facts & Biography." Live Science, Live Science, 13 Mar. 2014, www.livescience.com/44071-cleopatra-biography.html.

Penner, Jay. "Historical Accuracy of the Movie Scene of Cleopatra's Entry into Rome." Jaypenner.com, https://jaypenner.com/blog/the-cleopatra-procession-scene-historical-accuracy-and-realism.

Powers, Hermenia. "Cleopatra's Legacy in Art: Famous Pharaoh and Femme Fatale | Art UK." Artuk.org, 26 Mar. 2020, https://artuk.org/discover/stories/cleopatras-legacy-in-art-famous-pharaoh-and-femme-fatale.

"Ptolemaic Kingdom of Egypt | History Timeline." History Timelines, 2019, https://historytimelines.co/timeline/ptolemaic-kingdom-of-egypt. Accessed 6 Sept. 2024.

"Ptolemy XIII Theos Philopator | Macedonian King of Egypt." Encyclopedia Britannica, www.britannica.com/biography/Ptolemy-XIII-Theos-Philopator.

Robertson, Nan. "Claudette Colbert, 80 and Busy." New York Times, 16 Apr. 1984, pp. C-15, www.nytimes.com/1984/04/16/movies/claudette-colbert-80-and-busy.html. Accessed 6 Sept. 2024.

Saggu, Mehakpreet. "Cleopatra's Champagne." The Varsity, 4 Sept. 2023, https://thevarsity.ca/2023/09/04/cleopatras-champagne/. Accessed 6 Sept. 2024.

Schiff, Stacy. "Rehabilitating Cleopatra." Smithsonian, Smithsonian.com, Dec. 2010, www.smithsonianmag.com/history/rehabilitating-cleopatra-70613486/.

Shakespeare Birthplace Trust. "Antony and Cleopatra." Shakespeare Birthplace Trust, 2016, www.shakespeare.org.uk/explore-shakespeare/shakespedia/shakespeares-plays/antony-and-cleopatra/.

Sifuentes, Jesse. "The Propaganda of Octavian and Mark Antony's Civil War." World History Encyclopedia, 20 Nov. 2019, www.worldhistory.org/article/1474/the-propaganda-of-octavian-and-mark-antonys-civil/.

Stanley Mayer Burstein. The Reign of Cleopatra. Norman Univ. Of Oklahoma Press, 2007.

Strauss, Barry. "Cleopatra and Caesar." Barry Strauss, 5 July 2023, https://barrystrauss.com/cleopatra-and-caesar/.

---. "The Battle That Saddled Cleopatra with an Undeserved Bad Rep." The Daily Beast, 30 Mar. 2022, www.thedailybeast.com/the-battle-that-saddled-cleopatra-with-an-undeserved-bad-rep.

Strootman, Rolf. ANE Today – Cleopatra's Languages - American Society of Overseas Research (ASOR). 6 Feb. 2024, www.asor.org/anetoday/2024/02/cleopatras-languages.

Syed, Armani. "What the Debate over Cleopatra's "Race" Gets Wrong." Time, 20 Apr. 2023, https://time.com/6273435/cleopatra-race-debate-netflix/.

Thayer, Bill. "LacusCurtius • a Gateway to Ancient Rome."
Penelope.uchicago.edu,
http://penelope.uchicago.edu/Thayer/E/Roman/home.html

Translation source of : Plutarch, "Parallel Lives" and Dio Cassius "Roman
History."

Thayer, Bill, and B.L Ullman. Cleopatra's Pearls. Bill Thayer University of
Chicago, Feb. 1957,
https://penelope.uchicago.edu/Thayer/E/Journals/CJ/52/5/Cleopatras_Pearls*.
html. Accessed 5 Sept. 2024.

The Editors of Encyclopedia Britannica. "Ptolemy XII Auletes | Macedonian
King of Egypt." Encyclopedia Britannica, 15 Oct. 2009,
www.britannica.com/biography/Ptolemy-XII-Auletes.

"The Global Egyptian Museum | Buchis." Globalegyptianmuseum.org, 2024,
www.globalegyptianmuseum.org/glossary.aspx?id=98. Accessed 6 Sept. 2024.

Voight, Heather. "Cleopatra's Education." Heather on History, Heather on
History, 6 Feb. 2011, https://heathervoight.com/2011/02/06/cleopatras-
education/.

Wasson, Donald. "Caesar as Dictator: His Impact on the City of Rome."
World History Encyclopedia, 18 Jan. 2012,
www.worldhistory.org/article/112/caesar-as-dictator-his-impact-on-the-city-of-
rome/.

---. "Ptolemaic Dynasty." World History Encyclopedia, 29 Sept. 2016,
www.worldhistory.org/Ptolemaic_Dynasty/.

Watkins, Thayer. "The Timeline of the Life of Cleopatra." Sjsu.edu, 2020,
www.sjsu.edu/faculty/watkins/cleopatra.htm.

Welch, Craig. "How Volcanoes Caused Violent Uprisings in Cleopatra's
Egypt." Science, 17 Oct. 2017,
www.nationalgeographic.com/science/article/volcanoes-Nile-flood-climate-
Egypt.

"When Cleo Met Julius ... By Rolling Herself up in a Carpet." Google Arts &
Culture, https://artsandculture.google.com/story/when-cleo-met-julius-by-rolling-
herself-up-in-a-carpet-altes-museum-staatliche-museen-zu-
berlin/4QWxJNrY6GEQJQ?hl=en.

"When Cleopatra Visited Ancient Rome with Julius Caesar, All Hell Broke
Loose." History Skills, www.historyskills.com/classroom/ancient-
history/cleopatra-in-rome/.

Image Sources

1   https://commons.wikimedia.org/wiki/File:Ptolemy_XII_Auletes_Louvre_
    Ma3449.jpg

2   https://commons.wikimedia.org/wiki/File:Retrato_de_Julio_C%C3%A
    9sar_(26724093101).jpg

3   Byzantium565, CC BY-SA 4.0 <https://creativecommons.org/licenses/by-sa/4.0>,
    via Wikimedia Commons, https://commons.wikimedia.org/wiki/File:Octavian_
    and_Antony_denarius_(obverse).jpg

4   Alvaro qc by the original work of User:Husar de la Princesa, CC BY 2.5
    <https://creativecommons.org/licenses/by/2.5>, via Wikimedia Commons,
    https://commons.wikimedia.org/wiki/File:Roman_Republic_in_40bC.svg

5   https://commons.wikimedia.org/wiki/File:Woodcut_illustration_of_
    Cleopatra_and_Mark_Antony_-_Penn_Provenance_Project.jpg

6   https://commons.wikimedia.org/wiki/File:Posthumous_painted_
    portrait_of_Cleopatra_VII_of_Egypt,_from_Herculaneum,_Italy.jpg

7   https://commons.wikimedia.org/wiki/File:Kleopatra-VII.-Altes-Museum-Berlin1.jpg

8   https://commons.wikimedia.org/wiki/File:Tomb_of_Cleopatra_and_
    Mark_Antony,_illuminated_manuscript_of_Boccaccio,_miniature_by_the_Boucica
    ut_master,_1409_AD_(cropped).jpg

9   https://commons.wikimedia.org/wiki/File:Giampietrino_Death_of_Cleopatra.jpg

10 https://commons.wikimedia.org/wiki/File:Cleopatra_Bitten_By_an_Asp_
    MET_DP855160.jpg

11 https://commons.wikimedia.org/wiki/File:Guido_Reni_(Bologna_1575-
    Bologna_1642)_-_Cleopatra_with_the_Asp_-_RCIN_405338_-
    _Royal_Collection.jpg

12 https://commons.wikimedia.org/wiki/File:Cleopatra_-_John_William_Waterhouse.jpg

13 https://commons.wikimedia.org/wiki/File:Cleopatra_and_Caesar_by_Jean-Leon-Gerome.jpg

14 https://commons.wikimedia.org/wiki/File:Helen_Gardner_as_Cleopatra.jpg

15 https://commons.wikimedia.org/wiki/File:ThedaBara-Cleopatra.jpg

16 https://commons.wikimedia.org/wiki/File:Vivien_Leigh_-_Cleopatra.jpg

17 https://commons.wikimedia.org/wiki/File:Elizabeth_Taylor_Cleopatra_1963.JPG